"I believe that students with SLCN can be taught how to study and just like any other student they will learn skills... I think this resource is good for everybody not just SLCN students; it is adaptable and this is the key to it being a success."

Shirley Suleyman, Assistant SENCO

Study Skills for Students with SLCN

This highly practical resource has been designed to support professionals working with students who have SLCN (Speech, Language and Communication Needs) following a mainstream educational curriculum. Structured as a flexible 10-session programme, it takes a holistic approach to learning, encouraging students to take an active role in their studies by identifying individual learning strengths and building a "toolbox" of successful strategies for revision.

With photocopiable pages and downloadable resources, the advice and skills explored in this programme can be adapted to suit students with a range of abilities and incorporated into a timetable that can be used flexibly, over as many weeks as necessary, with very little planning required. Sessions focus on:

- Learning about revision and study methods, using a combination of visual, auditory and kinaesthetic techniques
- Creating a study skills folder and revision timetable
- Teaching command words (words used in exam questions) and exam preparation
- Building healthy study habits and managing anxiety
- Being proud of achievements and developing self-esteem
- Setting goals and becoming independent

Created to support a range of students, including those with a known diagnosis of autism, developmental language disorder, dyslexia, dyspraxia and attention deficit hyperactivity disorder, this is an invaluable resource for all professionals looking to support young adults with study skills in the build-up to exams.

Bhaveshi Kumar is a Specialist Speech and Language Therapist working for Sussex Community NHS Foundation Trust, in Brighton, UK. She graduated from City University, London in 2002, gaining a Masters in SLT in 2007. In her career she has worked as an NHS Therapist and independently both in the UK and abroad.

Bhaveshi works with a range of students who have speech, language and communication needs that are based in mainstream schools across Brighton and Hove. As part of a broad team linked to health and education services, a large part of her role includes supporting young people in schools and training education staff to deliver speech and language therapy plans and run targeted language groups based on students' needs. She is a member of the HCPC and RCSLT, and the sharing and development of skills and expertise relating to SLT across clients, families, educators and health professionals has been an intrinsic part of her role since she qualified.

Study Skills for Students with SLCN

A Group Programme Supporting Young Students Through Revision and Exams

Bhaveshi Kumar

First published 2020
by Routledge
2 Park Square, Milton Park, Abingdon, Oxon OX14 4RN

and by Routledge
52 Vanderbilt Avenue, New York, NY 10017

Routledge is an imprint of the Taylor & Francis Group, an informa business

© 2020 Bhaveshi Kumar

The right of Bhaveshi Kumar to be identified as author of this work has been asserted by her in accordance with sections 77 and 78 of the Copyright, Designs and Patents Act 1988.

All rights reserved. The purchase of this copyright material confers the right on the purchasing institution to photocopy or download pages which bear either the photocopy or eResources icon and a copyright line at the bottom of the page. No other parts of this book may be reprinted or reproduced or utilised in any form or by any electronic, mechanical, or other means, now known or hereafter invented, including photocopying and recording, or in any information storage or retrieval system, without permission in writing from the publishers.

Trademark notice: Product or corporate names may be trademarks or registered trademarks, and are used only for identification and explanation without intent to infringe.

British Library Cataloguing-in-Publication Data
A catalogue record for this book is available from the British Library

Library of Congress Cataloging-in-Publication Data
Names: Kumar, Bhaveshi, author.
Title: Study skills for students with SLCN : a group programme supporting young students through revision and exams / Bhaveshi Kumar.
Description: Abingdon, Oxon ; New York, NY : Routledge, 2020. | Includes bibliographical references.
Identifiers: LCCN 2019037267 (print) | LCCN 2019037268 (ebook) | ISBN 9781138387317 (paperback) | ISBN 9780429426346 (ebook)
Subjects: LCSH: Learning disabled children--Education (Secondary) | Children with disabilities--Education (Secondary) | Study skills. | Communicative disorders in children.
Classification: LCC LC4704.74 .K86 2020 (print) | LCC LC4704.74 (ebook) | DDC 371.9/0473--dc23
LC record available at https://lccn.loc.gov/2019037267
LC ebook record available at https://lccn.loc.gov/2019037268

ISBN: 978-1-138-38731-7 (pbk)
ISBN: 978-0-429-42634-6 (ebk)

Typeset in Avante Garde
by Servis Filmsetting Ltd, Stockport, Cheshire

Visit the eResources: www.routledge.com/9781138387317

Contents

	Foreword	ix
	My Background	x
	Acknowledgements	xi
	Study Skills for Students with SLCN	xii
	Definition of SLCN	xiii
	The Context	xiv
	Why Teach Revision and Study Skills?	xvi
	SLCN – A Unique Set of Skills	xvii
	The V A K Theory	xvii
	Who Will Benefit?	xx
	Evidence Base for Teaching Study Skills	xx
	The 10-Session Programme	xxi
	Overview of Sessions	xxii
	An Assistant SENCO's views	xxv
	Parents and Carers	xxvi
	A Parent's and Student's Views	xxvii
	Sonny's Baseline Assessment	xxviii
	Starting Point	xxx
	Notes	xxxi
SESSION 1	**Focus: Define Revision and Study Skills**	1
	Activity 1 Student Baseline Assessment	1
	Activity 2 Why Study?	1
	Activity 3 Revision Brainstorm	2
SESSION 2	**Focus: Visual (Looking), Auditory (Listening), Kinaesthetic (Doing)**	6
	Activity 1 Study Skills Folder	6
	Activity 2 How Do I Learn?	6
	Activity 3 Revision Practice	7
SESSION 3	**Focus: Visual (Looking)**	11
	Activity 1 Make a Flashcard	11
	Activity 2 Flashcard Competition	11
	Activity 3 Make a Mind Map	12

Contents

SESSION 4	**Focus: Auditory (Listening)**	**16**
	Activity 1 Make a Mnemonic	16
	Activity 2 Record It	16
	Activity 3 Discuss It	17
SESSION 5	**Focus: Kinaesthetic (Doing)**	**21**
	Activity 1 Make a Model	21
	Activity 2 Walk and Talk	21
	Activity 3 Sign It	22
SESSION 6	**Focus: Time and Time Concepts**	**26**
	Activity 1 The Time Game	26
	Activity 2 Make a Revision Timetable	26
	Activity 3 My Timeline	27
SESSION 7	**Focus: Exam Words (Command Words) – Complex Vocabulary**	**31**
	Activity 1 Exam Words (Command Words)	31
	Activity 2 Exam Words (Command Words): Word Search	31
	Activity 3 Multiple Meanings	32
SESSION 8	**Focus: Beat Exam Stress**	**36**
	Activity 1 The Exam and Access Arrangements	36
	Activity 2 Being Positive	36
	Activity 3 Mindfulness	37
SESSION 9	**Focus: Be Healthy**	**41**
	Activity 1 Healthy Habits Game	41
	Activity 2 Healthy Habits Poster	42
	Activity 3 Feed Your Brain	42
SESSION 10	**Focus: Evaluation and Moving Forward**	**46**
	Activity 1 V A K Recap	46
	Activity 2 Student Evaluation: My Personal Plan	46
	Activity 3 "Believe Everything Is Possible"	47
	Session Plan Resources	**51**
	Appendices	**105**
	Bibliography	**115**

Foreword

There are many young people who find it difficult to communicate with others, needing support to develop all the skills involved with communication. SLCN is the umbrella term most commonly used in schools to describe these difficulties, thus cutting through labels and diagnosis.

Children with SLCN may have difficulty with only one speech, language or communication skill or with several. Children may have difficulties with listening and understanding or with talking or both. Each child also has a unique combination of strengths. This means that every child with SLCN is different.

AFASIC 2019

My Background

As a Speech and Language Therapist I work in both primary and secondary settings, supporting a range of young students with speech, language and communication needs. Apart from Speech and Language Therapists, during my career I have worked alongside numerous professionals in both health and education including Specialist Special Educational Needs (SEN) Teachers, Educational Psychologists, Teachers, Teaching Assistants, EAL Teachers, Teachers of the Deaf, Occupational Therapists, Physiotherapists, Clinical Psychologists and Paediatricians.

I qualified as an SLT in 2002 and then went on to gain my Master's-level certificate in SLT at City University in London in 2007, I have also worked as an SLT in both the private and public sectors with opportunities to work in the UK and abroad. Prior to this I gained a BA Honours Degree in Humanities specialising in English and French literature at Nottingham Trent University. Previous work has also included working as a teacher for foreign language students in language schools both in the UK and in the USA.

Acknowledgements

Thanks to my work colleagues and friends in the SLT Team at Sussex Community NHS Foundation Trust and at the Brighton and Hove Inclusion Support Service (BHISS).

Special thanks for the help and advice given in putting this together from Matilda and Zeb Wileman, Shirley Suleyman, Pete Boyd, Caroline Coyne, Jim Elston, Claire Pimenta and Marie Newton whose support has been invaluable throughout this process.

Above all, thanks to my parents Bharat and Manjula, my sister Kaushal and my Aunt Hansa for all of their positivity and support since I embarked on this project.

Study Skills for Students with SLCN

All students benefit from being taught effective study skills. While there are many guides available to support students with study and revision, there are few that specifically cater to the needs of those with speech, language and communication needs.

In 2016 the Department of Health (DfE) statistics stated that of over 1.3 million children attending schools 15% had been identified as having some form of SLCN, and of these children 1.1 million attended mainstream schools in place of special schools.

Inclusion within a mainstream setting means these students will often access the same curriculum and exams as their more neurotypical peers. Whilst teachers make efforts to differentiate lessons to support their more diverse learning requirements, not having the equivalent support for study skills and revision in the long term puts those students who need it most at a higher risk of failing, impacting not just on their academic achievement but also on their motivation to learn and self-esteem.

This resource aims to fill this gap by empowering both students and those working alongside them to get explicitly involved in the revision and studying process. It encourages learners, and specifically those from neurodiverse populations, to explore different methods of revision and study practice through practical, fun and interactive approaches which are set out over a programme of 10 individual sessions.

Providing both an academic and functional focus, this allows students to develop study strategies that also match their communicative strengths, regardless of any diagnostic labels they may have been given, taking the often monotonous and anxiety-ridden ideas around studying or revision to a more positive, enjoyable and inspiring level.

Definition of SLCN

The words **Speech, Language** and **Communication** are often used interchangeably. The following provides a clear distinction between these terms.

Speech refers specifically to sounds produced orally, so includes the use of lips, tongue, palate and the vocal cords. These are the "sounds" that we make that form the language we use in sentences to express ourselves.

Language refers to the system of codes or symbols we use that make up words or sentences. It incorporates the shared rules we use to communicate with each other. Receptive language relates to the input side; the ability to hear, attend, discriminate, process, understand and retain the meanings that others have expressed. Expressive language is the ideas that are then transmitted into words that are then sequenced into a coherent and meaningful structure, e.g. through use of grammar. Language can be verbal or non-verbal, with the latter including all types of non-verbal communication such as eye blinking, signing or facial expression.

Communication refers to how we use our speech and language in a social context. It is broader than just speech or language as it includes all interactions we have with others. This encompasses all social and physical aspects of social communication such as eye contact, listening skills, conversation repair and emotional register.

Where a lack of any combination of the above skills has been identified there is a need for differentiated support. This identification of a "difference" at the outset is required before steps can be taken to adapt the learning environment to maximise a student's access to learning to achieve success.

The Context

In the UK around 8% to 16% of pupils have been reported to have some form of recognised SLCN.[1] Furthermore, it is likely that this is a gross under-representation of pupils seen in secondary settings with a figure closer to 40% of pupils when those who are not being identified are included. As many as 81% of students with emotional and/or behavioural difficulties are reported to have some form of SLCN that has not been identified. Outside of the UK, similar statistics of prevalence have been cited in countries such as the USA, Canada, Australia and New Zealand.[2] In the UK, this is reported to be further increased in students from socially disadvantaged backgrounds, with up to an average of 75% being recognised with low language levels in one inner city school[3] and about 50% in some areas of social deprivation.

Oral language skills such as vocabulary and narrative ability are known to be directly related to later academic success; vocabulary as early as age 5 is a strong predictor of literacy outcomes at age 11, vocabulary at age 13 often predicts how well a pupil is likely to succeed in GCSE Maths and English Literature. Being able to understand, retain and use vocabulary is often one of the key barriers to learning that students with SLCN have where they require the greatest support.

At secondary level the number of words students are required to learn daily increases. Taught vocabulary becomes more abstract or complex, with meanings that often change according to the subject; e.g. consider the words "mass", "wave" or "unit" and how these might have different meanings in different contexts, either socially or across different academic subjects such as English, Maths or Science. Language used in textbooks is also primarily written script, which is rarely explicit, with meanings harder to extract requiring more advanced ability in being able to infer and predict, as more abstract or sophisticated language is used.

Students are then expected to assimilate these words, concepts and ideas in lessons that are often crowded, fast-paced and sensorially challenging. Even when lessons are well differentiated and supported, students with SLCN, particularly those with auditory processing and memory difficulties, still have very little time to process, record and retain any verbal content taught which later need to be used for an essay or exam.

Focus in secondary schools is predominantly on literacy, with a lesser attention to supporting oral language.[4] Access to vocabulary at this stage therefore becomes primarily through reading, putting additional pressures on finding different ways for those with more limited reading skills to learn.

The Context

The Bercow Review stated that in 2018 only 20.3% of pupils with SLCN gained grade 4/C or above in English and Maths at GCSE compared with 63.9% of all pupils. This could potentially be linked to the alteration of the GCSE paper in 2017 which not only introduced a new grading system with tougher questions and more "rigorous content",[5] but linear rather than modular criteria for assessment. These changes potentially had two effects: firstly, that students who struggle with following and using vocabulary are being tested more intensely than the rest of the class due to those inherent challenges that learning and storing new vocabulary poses; and secondly, that additional pressures are added when students have to "cram" all of their revision practice into a single timeframe at the end of a year. This latter is a challenge for all students and not just those who have special educational needs.

Whilst this resource cannot alter the educational expectations of a mainstream curriculum and its testing procedures, it does address the need for a more bespoke approach to empowering these students by using "revision and study skills" as a platform which allows them to explore methods of learning successfully, enabling them to find different ways to retain what they learn and allowing some preparation for sitting exams. This is achieved by reinforcing the multisensory, practical and holistic methods involved in the process of studying which take into account the individual characteristics of the student, their motivations and their learning environments.

Why Teach Revision and Study Skills?

Essential study skills are very rarely explicitly taught in schools, which can be problematic for even the most able students. Yet there is increasing evidence to show that with effective study skills students can become more efficient, thoughtful and independent learners and perform better in school. Over time, this will no doubt increase chances of success and enable students to take greater advantage of learning opportunities.

When asked, most students struggle to define exactly what "revision" is. Revision is more than merely re-reading information. Revision is instead an act where students are encouraged to engage with learning material in a way that makes it meaningful, memorable and accessible later. The term "study skills" then becomes the broader remit, as apart from thinking about the best methods to revise, the student needs to think about the optimum conditions for revision, such as the environment they study in, the time allocated for study and their own physical and mental state to maximise chances of learning.

Students with SLCN are usually passive rather than active learners, relying on teachers or parents to regulate their studying in school and at home. Some of this may be attributed to learnt behaviour since many may have had full time 1:1 adult support throughout primary school thus finding it much harder to be independent when they reach secondary education. They also find it harder to monitor their understanding of content in lessons or self-monitor, with limited strategies in place to "fix" comprehension difficulties in the classroom, not understanding the real purpose of studying, or as mentioned earlier that they need to do more than just read content in order to understand and retain it.[6] The act of studying is also liable to be haphazard and disorganised as students with SLCN find it harder to keep track of materials and assignments and find it hard to finish work on time. Generally, students with SLCN are also likely to use a restricted range of study strategies, using the same study approach despite how effective it is, for all learning tasks irrespective of task content, structure or difficulty.

Revision and study skills therefore incorporate multiple facets not linked to recall of information alone. This resource will address different revision approaches, the purpose of study, time management and organisational skills and ways to encourage motivation. It also sets out to bring all those components together neatly into a programme that is practical and engaging for all students with a "can do" approach where they will develop functional skills and strategies they can hopefully continue to use beyond completion of the programme and through to tertiary education and college.

SLCN – A Unique Set of Skills

By the time students with SLCN reach secondary education many will have received a medical diagnosis that might help to explain their key areas of need. Those most widely seen in mainstream settings are autism, attention deficit hyperactivity disorder, dyslexia, dyspraxia and developmental language disorder alongside general learning or developmental difficulties and/or biomedical conditions such as Down syndrome or cerebral palsy amongst many others. Some of these students could also have an additional sensory impairment linked to a visual or hearing difficulty which can add to the potential learning challenges they encounter. Alongside such profiles will be students who have either gone undiagnosed, been misdiagnosed or have not met the specific criteria for a diagnostic label.

A "label" for most students will allow schools to fund their needs through additional educational advice and resources that some students may not get otherwise. Having a label, however, has different connotations to different students and families. For some it may have the negative effect of making them acutely aware of their differences and the amount of effort they might need to make daily to participate in usual, everyday learning tasks. Having a label can equally be empowering, helping some students to relate to the strengths that might be commonly associated with a condition, which when expressed positively gives the students a sense of identity, letting them open up and share commonalities with others who present similarly.

The group dynamic presented here will enable some discussion around so-called labels to take place. Fundamentally whilst similarities will exist amongst groups of learners, this programme still asserts the student as an individual and unique learner; with their own set of skills both social and academic, reinforcing that no two students will be the same and no two people will learn and work in the same way.

THE V A K THEORY: VISUAL (LOOKING), AUDITORY (LISTENING), KINAESTHETIC (DOING)

Historically it was assumed that individual students had one of three primary learning styles based on Visual, Auditory and Kinaesthetic styles known as the V A K learning styles theory.[7] Such theories have now either been discredited or have not yielded enough evidence to support their existence. Most people agree that a more holistic approach, incorporating all three of these modalities is required and that students can have different learning "abilities" but this is not linked to a learning style.[8]

SLCN – A Unique Set of Skills

Despite this, ideas linked to the V A K model works as a reflective exercise, allowing SLCN learners to hone their already established (or not) methods of learning. By categorising the different revision methods into each V A K category and choosing what works best, it is argued that they can start to build up their own "revision toolbox" and break any study habits that may have been ineffectual in the past. This resource makes it clear that while learning "styles" are not static or inherent, students with SLCN are still better adapted to a way of learning that matches the unique strengths they possess in their "diagnostic make-up". This could be through visual methods such as reading and pictures, auditory methods such as listening and discussion, or kinaesthetic methods such as gesture or building models with some adhering to all three.[9]

Strong evidence for learning abilities amongst various neurodiverse groups is also now available. Students with Down syndrome can struggle with auditory processing and comprehension so fare better with language tasks when their learning of vocabulary is supported using written scripts as they can be excellent at decoding.[10] For these students, revision methods such as writing words onto a flashcard, using mind maps and writing words onto sticky notes will play to their reading strengths thus helping them remember key facts and vocabulary.

A student with dyslexia who struggles to read could instead use the method of audio-recording keywords or concepts; alternatively they may be better at using other more creative approaches to learning such as artwork and drawing, to serve as a memory aid. Research has pointed to dyslexic learners often being creative. A study conducted in Malaysia investigated the making of letters and words using clay as having a significantly positive effect on reading compared to a more traditional method of using phoneme awareness. Success comes from turning their perceived disadvantage into their strength as they seek different and creative ways to problem solve and overcome difficulties. This suggests that there is some mileage in thinking "outside the box" to reach groups of people where traditional methods of learning may have failed them.

Another example is a student with a developmental language disorder who struggles with both vocabulary storage and word retrieval, who is likely to gain more using a visual or semantic approach such as a word map with categories to support their mental storage of new words. Here they might write the word's function / its group name / synonym (similar word) / antonym (opposite word) to facilitate its retention and recall in an exam situation. These students will often be motivated by rewards so having more frequent reward systems in place, e.g. on their revision timetable, might also work better to encourage them.

The examples above are illustrations as every student will not easily fit into these conjectures or fit a stereotype that is necessarily attached to a label given. An example might be a student with autism. Such individuals are often perceived to be visual learners so many of the visual approaches mentioned would be effective, although some may initially struggle with visual approaches because of a more prominent sensory integration difficulty. In this instance a kinaesthetic approach to revision which incorporates movement such as the **Walk and Talk** method where the student rehearses a word whilst walking around the room, would work, directly supporting their need for movement stimulation and in turn possibly decreasing any anxiety as they are given an activity to focus on. Equally they might be further aided in their revision by adapting their revision plan so that it includes more regular sensory breaks with activities which will help them to relax and self-regulate at home, making it easier for them to revise and learn information more effectively when they come to it.

This resource allows students, no matter what diagnosis, to experiment with different methods of learning that support retention of information and revision, with a shared functional focus in finding out which methods work and can be used to their advantage.

It also asserts that students are generally unaware of the best approach until they have had some opportunities to practise a range of approaches and execute at least one of them well. An example is when a student is asked what they do to "revise" their response might be "use flashcards", but when asked to make a flashcard, they write the keyword in one corner of the card, e.g. respiration, then they produce eight lines of writing on the same side of the card to define the word, all in one colour, very small and difficult to read. Whilst copying the information from a book or a screen, they have not really been paying attention to the key points they have listed or thought about how easy or difficult it might be to read and memorise all that information once it was written down.

Evidently this student will have more success in learning the definition of respiration through adapting their flashcard, by eliminating some of the writing, sticking to one or two key points, using different colours and adding pictures or symbols that will help as an *aide memoire* at a later date.

Working in a group not only offers opportunities to draw on skills but also allows students to develop bonds with one another through discovery of shared interests and development of all the prerequisite skills we use socially. This would include listening, eye contact, turn-taking and conversational skills, as well as giving an opinion and showing respect for others' contributions and insights. In addition to social communication skills, the group dynamic also lends itself to developing a greater sense of self-awareness and self-advocacy as they get better at describing what they identify with and what works or doesn't work for them.

Who Will Benefit?

This resource is aimed at speech therapists, specialist teachers, teaching assistants and other educators working directly with secondary students and those with SLCN. The studying principles are, however, adaptable and can be made relevant to all students who are required to revise and perform in exam situations. This includes those being home schooled, those in post-16 education establishments, and those attending youth offending institutions and pupil referral units, amongst others.

This resource could also be used more widely, with students struggling with emotional or behavioural issues, as well as those with English as an additional language who might benefit from explicit guidance on revision that is simple and clear to understand. Having the motivation to revise is a challenge for all students. This resource develops this by creating a positive, inspiring and fun platform to approach study skills and revision, giving students opportunities to embrace those learning challenges openly.

EVIDENCE BASE FOR TEACHING STUDY SKILLS

Implicitly teaching study skills has been shown to improve academic performance.[11] A previous study done in the US subscribes to this idea, reporting that study skills are linked to four essential clusters: *repetition or rehearsal strategies, procedural or organisation-based study skills, cognitive-based study skills and metacognitive-based study skills*. The areas are described as follows:

1. *Repetition-based study skills* are where the student is asked to repeat words or facts over and over, this method being mostly successful when trying to learn small bits of information in the short term, e.g. a list of words, a list of spellings or maths equations. It has been proven to be successful when adding mnemonics, e.g. a mental image or picture.

2. *Procedural-based study skills* are linked to the individual becoming organised, linked to time management, developing study routines and having a revision timetable.

3. *Cognitive-based study skills* are the use of semantic word maps or mind maps where the student might need to learn a larger amount of content, e.g. think about written texts linked to English or History. Here they learn and recall the information needed through making visual representations of the key ideas and themes that can be interconnected.

4. *Metacognitive-based study skills* are where a student can assess their own need for studying so they can evaluate their own performance making adaptations and changes as they go along.

All four of these evidence-based approaches are used and expanded on within the content of this programme.

The 10-Session Programme

The intervention programme is divided into 10 weekly sessions. Each session is dedicated to one key area of focus around study skills and revision strategies. Each comes with an illustrated overview of the targets that are covered in each week, step-by-step instructions on how to deliver each activity and a key for where the activity resources can be found in the manual. A template where the session can be recorded is also offered at the back of the manual.

The timing of 10 sessions over 10 weeks is based on a pupil attending a double lesson of 90 minutes, which could be the case in a mainstream secondary school. The material lends itself to being spread over two single 50-minute lessons a week over 5 weeks, or one 50-minute session conducted over a fortnight over 2 terms. Its use will largely depend on the ability range of students, availability of staff and whether some areas of revision and study skills need a more intense focus. For example, the facilitator may want to spend a longer period of time on developing the specific revision strategies or want to focus just on exam preparation or on being healthy, having a positive mindset and practising relaxation techniques.

The programme is designed to support groups of students learning together, although many of the strategies could be followed up during individual sessions with a student or be supported in pairs.

The content within the programme is unique as it adapts to suit a range of students, offering enough versatility to be incorporated into most secondary student timetables over as many weeks as is required. A follow-up activity at the end of each session will also give the students a chance to consolidate any new learning and ensures that there is some generalisation of skills that can take place outside of the group, which can then allow parents and caregivers to be a part of this empowering experience.

Overview of Sessions

Session 1

A student baseline assessment is completed at the beginning of the group, where students can identify and discuss what they know about revision and share information about who helps them to study at home and at school.

The initial session is aimed at group cohesion and the students getting to know each other. Whilst sharing their responses about revision and study practice, the session provides an opportunity for them to identify and share the name of a key person who can assist them when help is required, making them feel safe in the process of asking for support throughout the revision and study process. Students with SLCN find both independent learning and asking for help hard so introducing this at the start gives the student the reassurance that support will be available for them both in and out of school. The support they receive may not be from a parent but could be from an older sibling, relative, teacher, home tutor or friend. The facilitator can support the student at this stage to find out who that key person is if the student cannot think of a suitable person.

Session 2

The next session moves on to the individual's own motivations for studying, prompted by assembling the students' individual statements. It is interesting to see how different students' motivations vary in this case; e.g. for some the priority is that they can go to a college of their choice so they get a job they want, for others it could be to learn new things. Students with SLCN can find it hard to think outside of the moment, so this also allows them to start to think independently about future desires and how study skills could be a very small part of achieving their own personal goals.

Thinking about why we learn what we learn, is part of a metacognitive approach that runs throughout the programme. There has been research to show that metacognition[12] and self-regulation approaches show high levels of impact in terms of educational progress and, for schools, is one of the most cost-effective approaches when considering budgets and deployment of staff. The research also indicates that any strategies employed are even more effective when taught in collaborative groups, so that learners can be supported by their peers and make their thinking explicit through discussion. These approaches are known to be particularly effective for low-achieving and older pupils, highlighting how essential this is for supporting study skills with teenagers who may be feeling demoralised by their failures. Fundamentally it encourages students to become comfortable with talking to others about what works for them, acknowledging any personal struggles in learning so that they can take the next step in improving their situation should they need to.

Overview of Sessions

A study skills folder is introduced at this point so they can start to keep the resources they create over the next 8 sessions. The folder could contain the following materials: sticky notes to support visual methods of revision and keyword learning; A4 paper for creating mind maps and word maps; coloured pens and index cards to make flashcards; highlighters so they can draw attention to keywords they need to learn; magnets to enable students to attach revision timetables on a fridge at home; moulding putty to support making models that can replicate a keyword or concept required.

This list is not exhaustive and can be adapted for the individual needs of the students in the group as is appropriate to that student; e.g. it could include a smart pen which highlights and spells the written word for the student who is dyslexic, or it could contain a talking tin which has a simple recording device for students with fine-motor coordination difficulties with dyspraxia or a fidget ball which alleviates stress helping a student with ADHD to self-regulate. Students are encouraged to personalise their folders at this stage and add things that they know to be useful. The folders should be kept in a safe place at school where they be accessed frequently, along with any resources created during the group.

Sessions 3, 4 and 5

The next three sessions of the group are dedicated to continuing to develop the students "revision toolbox". This entails going through examples of some fun and inspiring ways to revise under the headings of **Visual** (**Looking**), **Auditory** (**Listening**) and **Kinaesthetic** (**Doing**) in turn. They have opportunities to practice different revision skills in each area so that they start to learn new strategies or enhance the ones they already have, building up their skills in learning the methods that match their strengths and abilities.

Session 6

The understanding of time concepts is explored. Students are also given opportunities to create and develop their own revision timetables. Many students with SLCN struggle with time and organisation skills so this session allows them to think about organising their time and plan for future events. The concept of time also directly relates to the students' understanding of the passing of time and how this might relate to them planning their answers under timed conditions, e.g. when in an exam. This session also covers vocabulary which is linked to time concepts which students who have SLCN often find difficult.

Sessions 7 and 8

Difficulties with vocabulary and particularly with complex tier-two words[13] are introduced next, moving onto understanding the language used in exam questions. If students do not understand the subtle differences between words such as "argue", "explain", "summarise" and "compare" they will struggle with answering exam questions correctly, leading them to lose marks or fail. These are known as "command" words and here provides an opportunity where their meanings are taught explicitly in the group. The idea of understanding and retaining complex vocabulary is further developed here through looking at specific curriculum words

Overview of Sessions

that can often be difficult, paying attention to words with double meanings that students can sometimes confuse, e.g. words like "text", "bracket", "wave" or "present".

There may be students in the group who also have access arrangements, but are unaware of what they are, or are unsure about how to use this to their advantage during their exams. For the large majority, access arrangements might not have been granted, so for these students the focus is given on the time in exams being used wisely, thinking about how they can prepare best for sitting the paper.

Session 8 is also dedicated to dealing with stress and looks at developing a positive mindset. Research into the concept of neuroplasticity states the teenage brain is in a constant changing state with the identification of a "pruning" process of neurons and connections within the brain that are not being used during the teenage years to a strengthening of those that are.[14] A study has documented that both visual-spatial memory and cognitive ability is improved in adolescents aged 11–20 years and this has been linked to this maturation process.[15] With older students who have SLCN the concept of neuroplasticity provides hope as the conventional view has been that if students have not achieved their "potential" by the time they reach secondary education they never will. The so called "critical period" which was said to be just in the early years is now shown to extend until much later, and up to at least 17 years of age.[16]

The concept of neuroplasticity closely links to the evidence associated with mindfulness practice. Recent research has also shown that those with the lowest levels of executive control and emotional stability are the ones who are most likely to benefit most from mindfulness training. Whilst we are unable to class all students with SLCN into this category, there is certainly enough evidence on mindful practices to the point where it is now commonly included in many medical as well as psychological practices as an evidence-based research.

Stress can negatively impact on maturation of the brain areas so mindfulness learning interventions which improve executive function also support stress reduction, and therefore are likely to lead to better academic improvements. One evaluation of children with learning difficulties showed significantly improved academic achievement and social skills through mindfulness training. It would therefore seem appropriate that this is introduced here as a method which can potentially improve study skills through increasing optimum mental health and wellbeing which supports learning.

Session 9

Research increasingly suggests that living a healthier lifestyle can significantly improve cognitive ability. Specific areas of focus in this session are the benefits of brain boosting foods (as part of a healthy, balanced diet), the importance of a regular sleep pattern and the need for regular exercise. This is also an area where students and families can exert a level of control and forms part of the overall process of maximising revision and study skills practice.

Overview of Sessions

It is fundamental throughout the intervention programme to reassure students that there is no such thing as "perfect" with the focus placed on effort and trying one's best. This programme is ultimately about developing skills that they can use throughout their lives and improving their resilience and their ability to feel a level of control is a large part of them achieving success.

Session 10

In the final session the progress of each pupil is reviewed. This session not only revisits the revision methods previously encountered but will include the students creating a personal plan as they think about their next steps forward. A rating scale is also employed to define outcome measures that can be recorded and shared by educators and sent to parents and caregivers.

The session ends on celebrating success and challenges overcome by role models in the media or in history. Celebrities or icons that are familiar can be introduced here such as Albert Einstein for autism or David Beckham for dyslexia. Or there may be others that are more popular or relevant to the group, based on an aspect of their study. With more able students you might even engage them with the My Label and Me advice sheets to see how they view the different profiles and whether they can relate to the descriptions given and whether or not they agree to them.

Developing social independence and inspiration to succeed are aims that should always be at the core of any long-term communication plan when working with young adults. This programme addresses these throughout, looking at how students are motivated and what "success" might mean directly to them. It will explore how these students can then be supported in some way to see beyond the day-to-day learning platform, to a world where education has been provided for a purpose, enabling them to think beyond their current schooling and into their personal futures.

AN ASSISTANT SENCO'S VIEWS

Experiences of Teaching Study Skills to SLCN Students in Mainstream Schools

In my experience I have often found that a lot of students firstly do not know what revision is, they think that just reading their work is revising. I will try to teach them what this means and, overall, I think that my experience of teaching study skills has shown to be effective. One strategy I use is to allow my students to mind map their revision onto an A4 sheet; here we have discussed each strategy of learning on the mind map in detail. I have also introduced the use of a highlighter with one student where she was taught to highlight specific words that were tricky in maths then look the words up; for her this not only increased her awareness of the vocabulary she did not know but it also gave her a strategy that was instrumental in alleviating her anxiety, as in exams she had "something" she knew she could do, i.e. highlight, giving her a purpose.

Overview of Sessions

I believe that students with SLCN can be taught how to study just like any other student and they will learn skills. The difficulty with such students, however, is being able to use these skills independently; this is harder. The current education system is also not set up to really help these students when it comes to examinations, as although access arrangements can benefit a student with SLCN, this is often not enough; e.g. students who need constant prompting in class; aren't allowed to be prompted in exams, and this then leads to failures. There could be more done to enable those students therefore before they get to the exams. Having effective study skills and revision strategies which include exam question practice may be one way to do this. In my experience few students take entry-level exams when in mainstream settings and most of them work towards GCSEs.

Exams are hard for these students as they often use tier-two vocabulary, words like evaluate, summarise, explain, which are all abstract and very subtle in difference. The language used in exams is also geared towards students having to infer and predict from texts and although the student might be able to give an exact narrative of what happened in a text, the difficulties they have in understanding the convoluted wording of exam-type questions means that this will also lead to failures. More could be taught on how to tackle exam-type questions with these students.

I think that this resource is good for everybody, not just SLCN students. Trying to do interventions in schools is hard for many reasons; the pupils need to be withdrawn from class, a room needs to be found and resources need to be gathered. Having the right teaching assistant who can be trained to deliver the intervention also needs to be considered. This resource offers advice in all of these areas and above all it is adaptable; this is key to it being a success.

PARENTS AND CARERS

At the start of the programme, parents and carers are informed about their teenager's participation along with information on the key areas covered and the potential benefits the intervention will have. Parents and carers will often have the most influence on how the student revises as the notion of revision and study skills is that the majority of this takes place outside of school and usually in the home environment.

Many parents and carers often struggle to communicate with their teenager and having a conversation with a young adult with SLCN can be harder still, because of the additional speech, language and communication barriers. It is fundamental to ensure that both the students and their parents or carers can discuss revision and study skills and find ways to approach this at home. This intervention allows for this to happen by enabling there to be a situation where such discussion can be stimulated. For this reason involvement of parents is requested at the start of the intervention with a parent letter which explains the intervention programme and the areas that will be covered. Each week also offers a follow-up activity which students can take home, to share with parents and to consolidate any learning practices from the group.

Overview of Sessions

A PARENT'S AND STUDENT'S VIEWS

The following is a discussion with Mia, the mother of a 15-year-old student called Sonny, and her experiences with Sonny's study habits and revising techniques.

Sonny's journey through both primary and secondary education offered challenges. The outcomes of various assessments administered by Educational Psychologists/Speech therapists and Dyslexia Specialists over the years described him with a mixed profile of skills with features of dyslexia, dyspraxia, developmental language disorder, auditory processing and cognitive delay, but not "enough" in any area to give him a specific diagnosis or to warrant an Education and Health Care Plan (EHCP) plan which might have provided extra support for him at school.

Interview with Mia

BK: *How do you approach revision and study skills with Sonny at home?*

M: *It is often very sporadic; I approach it nervously. I might have a plan and will try to do it that way although this does not always work. I always try to give him notice too. I try to suggest something manageable, but this is usually met with strong emotion and a definite 'no'. When I feel this resistance, I can then find my concerns and worries rise to the surface and the discussion isn't as relaxed as I hoped. Most of the revision we have done is when he wants to do it, rather than when I've suggested it. He will usually ask when he feels he must, that his teachers are telling him he must. etc.*

BK: *What are the strategies that currently work?*

M: *Mind maps? Discussing around a topic, e.g. with History, talking about the context, the people, the experiences. Using images/creating posters.*

BK: *What are the challenges of trying to encourage Sonny to study at home?*

M: *We have done very little revision together. Revision is a reminder of school and feeling inadequate, which brings up a lot of emotions and, if possible, he would rather avoid it. I noticed at the end of summer holidays, after 6 weeks off, we worked on a piece of work reviewing his History mock and he was relaxed and engaged.*

BK: *Do you have a revision/study timetable in place?*

M: *No. I have tried/suggested but he says he prefers not to.*

BK: *How do you ensure the health and wellbeing of Sonny when he is not at school?*

M: *Be available to talk when he wants to. Check in with him. Try to go for a walk together. Encourage him.*

BK: *Does Sonny have friends that they can study with?*

M: *This has never been something he would consider.*

Overview of Sessions

BK: *What is Sonny's general attitude towards studying at home?*

M: *Pained. He wants to do it as quickly as possible. The whole experience seems to feel like a reminder of what he can't do.*

BK: *Are there any specific areas you would like more support with so that Sonny's motivation to study and their ability to study is more successful?*

M: *For revision/studying not to be so painful. For him to feel he has his own strengths. To find techniques that inspire him. To help us find some structure in our revision. To have a plan that works for us.*

SONNY'S BASELINE ASSESSMENT

1. Revision and study skills are *gathering information together for an exam.*
2. I know how to revise for exams. *Sonny was asked to give a number using a scaling system of 0 to 10 with 10 being the best. He gave himself a score of 4.*
3. At school if I need help, *I can ask my history teacher, as we have a book/buddy/board system.*
4. At home if I need help, *I can get help from my mum, sometimes my dad but my dad finds it hard so usually my mum.*
5. I will usually study *in my bedroom; it is in the attic so it is far away from everyone.*
6. If I come across 1 tricky word *I can look it up on the internet.*
7. When I leave school *I want to be an illustrator.*

The above illustrates how some of the challenges of revision at home can manifest. Many parents experience something similar to Mia when trying to manage expectations of homework and exam revision. Sonny is a mature, able and motivated student, the discussion with the parent and baseline questionnaire helped us to uncover studying techniques that could be improved to make studying and revision more fun and appealing. This included thinking about the environment within which study takes place: e.g. was the bedroom best, or would he be better at the library or in a cafe, giving Sonny the opportunity to make more independent choices on how to learn or which strategies worked best for him to use. We also discussed him experimenting with new things such as studying with a partner. The most important outcome was for parent and child to have regular and honest dialogue on both sides about aspects that did or did not work throughout that period.

Sonny was interviewed again at the end of his GCSEs, after acting on some of the methods we highlighted. Sonny reported the following:

Overview of Sessions

Revision was ok in the end. I didn't realise that I could use the things that I enjoyed, like art and drawing to help me revise: it made it fun! (*This was immediately a remedy to his mother's views on how the very idea of studying was laden with anxiety for Sonny and his own views on how he rated his ability to revise, which was at a 4.*)

I enjoyed History, we did the date in big writing and I put the mind maps on the landing, I liked the post it notes idea but they kept falling off! I put things on the fridge, but that didn't work for me as I forgot to look there, so I moved them to the door on my wardrobe. (*The process of using something he "enjoyed" like art allowed him to become more creative with his studying and find "new" ways he had not considered to help him revise; he realised that placing his revision notes on the fridge was not something that worked for him.*)

I felt better about going into exams the more I did it but I hate it when everyone talks about it afterwards. When I get to school before an exam it is nice when teachers talk to you and wish you luck; everyone is really friendly before the exam, which helps me feel calm. (*He was looking more closely at what made him feel anxious or calm and recognised that having that reassurance from an adult at school was helpful at the start of the exam day.*)

My mum has been really helpful, but I think I prefer to work on my own sometimes; it can be stressful if she is stressed. I know she wants to help me: she works in a college so she knows what it's like! (*Sonny was able to articulate this and show a wider capacity for thinking, showing empathy for his mother and showing self-awareness, i.e. that he could reduce both his and his mother's anxiety, e.g. by working alone on some occasions.*)

For Sonny improvement was about having the "I can" approach. It was about making tweaks in his revision approaches and adaptations to how he might study that were effective. He knew that others were also there to provide support and understanding.

Starting Point

The following chapters will go through the 10 sessions in detail with simple instructions on how to deliver the individual group sessions. The focus of each week is clearly identified with the required materials for each group listed with page references so that the facilitator can be guided to where the resources can be found.

Colour resources are available to download on the Routledge website. Facilitators can also use symbols and pictures from sources that students are already familiar with.

A brief methodology is outlined to go with each activity, with a session notes template in the appendices where each session can be documented so the facilitator has a reminder of who has attended, the key areas which have been covered, whether the learning aims for each activity were met by the individual student and where to go next.

To ensure that students are attentive and engaged means that each week starts with a warm-up game. Games are also listed in the appendices that can be used to engage students at the beginning of each session. The sessions follow the same sequence each week so that students know what to expect. Although the warm-up games are different each week, there is no real reason why the same games cannot be used more than once to ensure that there is greater consistency and familiarity. Students' enjoyment of the activities will sustain their engagement and build into their sense of belonging to the group. Feeling comfortable will relieve any anxieties they have too, allowing for a better uptake of skills and a bigger impact on emotional wellbeing.

The group space that they work in needs to remain consistent and free from any outside distractions, whether this is noise or other students using the same room. Try to also make sure that the room is booked in advance for the duration of the sessions required. In secondary schools this can be problematic, so it is always advised that this is done at the beginning to avoid too many changes in the longer term.

Choose students who are in the same year groups, with no more than 8 to 10, so that the content can match what they might be learning in the curriculum. For example, if the student is in Year 10 and learning *Macbeth*, the revision methods could be tailored to that subject alone for the entirety of the programme, meaning the materials created to develop their revision skills are relevant and functional as well as having the benefit of increasing their skills and abilities.

Keep the mood of the group light and fun, you might also want to create some group rules at the start of the session that everyone can contribute to. Always make sure that the study skills folders are available at the start of each session.

Notes

1. Sage, R. (2005) "Communicating with Students Who Have Learning and Behaviour Difficulties: A Continuing Professional Development Programme", *Emotional and Behavioural Difficulties*, Vol. 10, No. 4. pp. 282–297.
2. McLeod, S. & McKinnon, D. H. (2007) "The Prevalence of Communication Disorders Compared with Other Learning Needs in 14,500 Primary and Secondary School Students", *International Journal of Language and Communication Disorders*, Vol. 42 (S1), pp. 37–59. http://www.peispeechhearing.ca/admin/Editor/assets/speechhearingfactsheet.pdf.
3. Jean Gross Communication Champion 2011, The Communication Trust (see www.communication.trust.org.uk).
4. Joffe. V (2015). "An International Perspective: Supporting Adolescents with Speech, Language, and Communication Needs in the United Kingdom", *Seminars in Speech and Language*, Vol. 36, No. 1, pp. 74–86. doi: 10.1055/s-0034-1396448.
5. CIFE (2018) "Problems with the New GCSE Exams", 29 July. https://www.cife.org.uk/article/problems-new-gcse-exams.
6. Gettinger, M. (2002) "Contributions of Study Skills to Academic Competence", *Seibert School Psychology Review*, Vol. 31, No. 3, pp. 350–365.
7. Gholami S and Bagheri M S (2013) "Relationship between VAK Learning Styles and Problem Solving Styles regarding Gender and Students' Fields of Study", *Journal of Language Teaching and Research*, Vol. 4 No. 4, pp. 700–706.
8. Willingham, D. T. (2015) "The Scientific Status of Learning", *Styles Theories*, Vol. 42, No. 3, pp. 266–271.
9. Baghat, Rashmi Vyas & Tejinder Singh (2015) "Students' Awareness of Learning Styles and Their Perceptions to a Mixed Method Approach for Learning", *International Journal of Applied Basi Medical Research*, Vol. 5 (Suppl. 1), S58–S65.
10. Willingham, D. T. (2015) "The Scientific Status of Learning," *Styles Theories*, Vol. 42, No. 3, pp. 266–271.
11. Baghat, Rashmi Vyas & Tejinder Singh (2015) "Students Awareness of Learning Styles and Their Perceptions to a Mixed Method Approach for Learning". *International Journal of Applied Basi Medical Research*, Vol. 5 (Suppl. 1), S58–S65.
12. Lo, Sao Cheong (2011) "Effects of the Clay Modelling Program on the Reading Behavior of Children with Dyslexia: A Malaysian Case Study", *The Asia Pacific Education*, November.
13. Beck, Isabel L., Margaret G. McKeown & Linda Kucan (2013) *Bringing Words to Life Robust Vocabulary Instruction*. New York: Guilford Press. 2nd Edition.
14. See https://www.memory-key.com/memory/development/child/adolescent.
15. Burggraaf, Rudolf, Maarten A. Frens, Ignace T. C. Hooge & Jos N. Van der Geest (2018) "Performance on Tasks of Visuospatial Memory and Ability: A Cross-sectional Study in 330 Adolescents Aged 11 to 20", *Applied Neuropsychology: Child*, Vol. 7, No. 2, pp. 129–142.
16. Hartshorne, J. K. (2018) "A Critical Period for Second Language Acquisition: Evidence from 2/3 Million English Speakers", *Cognition*. Vol. 177 pp. 263–277.

Session 1

Focus: Define Revision and Study Skills

The purpose of this session is to define the terms "revision" and "study skills". Revision refers to the strategies we employ when going over learning material so that it can be understood, retained and recalled at a future time; specifically, for the purpose of passing a test or exam. Study skills are the context within which we might revise, thinking more about how we study effectively, e.g. effective time management, creating the right working environment, ensuring the right materials are to hand, and maintaining health and personal wellbeing to maximise our chances of learning.

The focus of the first session is on introducing the concept of revision and study skills to gain a baseline assessment of the student's ideas on what revision and study means to them, who their key support person might be at school or at home and what career hopes they might have for the future at this point.

Activity 1 Student Baseline Assessment

A student baseline assessment is introduced to students. Each question should be read out clearly with students writing their responses. Students who struggle with reading and writing will need additional assistance with this. Once everyone has completed the baseline, the facilitator can ask the students to share their answers in the group.

Activity 2 Why Study?

Students are given a list of statements that they need to put into order of importance, the most important being at the top. The purpose of this exercise is for them to start thinking about what motivates them to study and do well at school. Some of these students may never have revised so it is important to explain clearly *what* revision is, and *why* students might revise, e.g. so that *we remember our learning, we understand and remember tricky words, we follow our lessons better or we do better in exams.*

Session 1

Once each student has completed the activity the facilitator can take a picture of their statements and print them, serving as a point of reference in the following sessions. The picture of their statements could equally be put up on a wall that has been dedicated to the theme of study skills, e.g. in the common room or main classroom where they are likely to spend the most time. The statements are given to them as a reminder in Session 2 where they can add these to the new study skills folders that they create.

Activity 3 Revision Brainstorm

The facilitator writes *REVISION* on the middle of a whiteboard or on to an A2 or A3 sheet of paper to create a mind map. Students are asked to call out or write one revision method they are aware of and the facilitator adds this to the map. Here, the facilitator may want to pick some key methods from the revision methods examples in the resource to initiate further responses. The facilitator's role is to encourage the students to think about things they might have done before to help them remember their learning.

By the end of this session, enough information will have been gathered to initiate student discussion on aspects that are already working or not working for them and ones that might be unique to some students, e.g. *Jamie likes to watch YouTube videos to help him remember facts about a subject,* or *Maya looks up words using Google but reading some of the words can be tricky.* The group can then be prompted to think about whether these are the best strategies for them or whether there are others that they could use which are more useful or appealing.

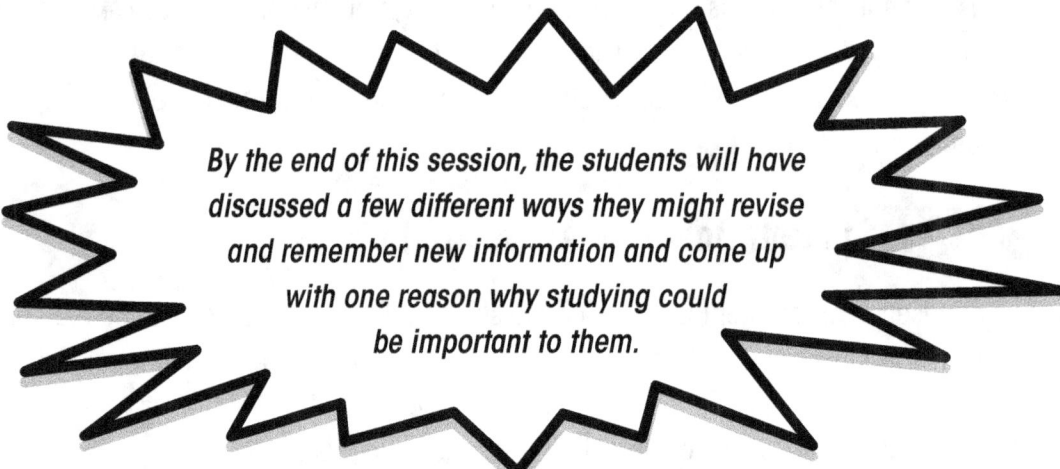

By the end of this session, the students will have discussed a few different ways they might revise and remember new information and come up with one reason why studying could be important to them.

Session 1

Session Plan 1 — Warm-up Game p. 107 / Resources 1 pp. 52–54

Area of focus: Define Revision and Study Skills		
Warm-up Game	**Game: Spin the Bottle**	
Activity	**Task**	**Materials/Resources needed**
1	**Student Baseline Assessment** The baseline is handed out. The facilitator should read the questions out first, then give each student the questionnaire to fill in. The facilitator should assist those students who need support with reading or writing their answers. The answers can then be shared in the group.	Student Baseline Assessment. Pens.
2	**Why Study?** A set of statements are given out and each student puts their statements into order of preference with the most important at the top.	Copies of Why Study? statements are cut out/laminated and placed in front of each student. A tablet/smartphone may be required to take a photograph of each student's list, which is then added to their folders in Session 2.
3	**Revision Brainstorm** Students list in turn what they are doing already to revise. If they cannot think of anything the facilitator can list some methods which might be familiar already, e.g. make a flashcard. Students discuss things that work well or do not work well. To make this more interactive, the students can be asked to individually write their answer onto the paper or whiteboard.	A2 or A3 sheet of paper/whiteboard to record students' contributions. The facilitator saves this piece of work ready for the following session where this is reintroduced after the concepts of the V A K are examined.
Follow-up Activity	Students are told to choose one revision method they know already to practise and share with the group in Session 2.	

Session 1

Follow-up 1:

Students practise one way to revise that has been discussed and share this with the group the following week.

Session 1

FOLLOW-UP 1 NOTES

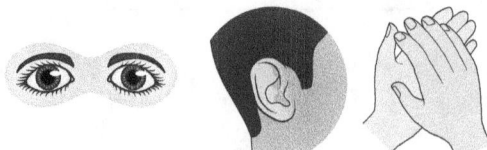

Session 2

Focus: Visual (Looking), Auditory (Listening), Kinaesthetic (Doing)

The focus of this session is to primarily introduce the student's study skills folders and then to look specifically at how different methods of revision can be allocated to the three primary senses we use to acquire information. These primary senses are **Visual**, **Auditory** and **Kinaesthetic**. Talking about learning in this way enables the student to become focused on *how* we can potentially learn using our different senses. Students with SLCN can be taught different ways of learning specific to their individual abilities and preferences.

Activity 1 Study Skills Folder

The study skills folder is introduced. The student should refer to this throughout the coming weeks with support from the facilitator to make sure it is physically accessible and referred to as often as possible. This should be presented in every session and each time the student is set a learning task where any type of recording or revision is required. Any revision aids that are produced either in the group or in individual sessions with that student can then be added to the folder.

It is advisable that the folder stays at the main educational base as there is a risk that students will lose them if they take them home. The usefulness of the folder depends on the encouragement given by educators, parents and carers in maintaining it and using it as often as possible. Personalising the folder and making it colourful and decorative should be encouraged so that students are motivated to use them. Any time dedicated to this would be time well spent.

Activity 2 How Do I Learn?

The concept of how we learn is introduced: are we primarily **Visual** and learn through looking and images, are we mostly **Auditory** and rely on listening and sounds or are we **Kinaesthetic**, learning more by actions and movement?

Session 2

The students are presented with a survey made up of multiple-choice questions about a situation that best resonates with them. Each statement is based on either a **Visual, Auditory** or **Kinaesthetic** experience. This process helps them identify the different sensory channels that can support different ways of learning. This is not necessarily about "owning a style" and in most cases there may be more than one example that they relate to.

It is important to explain that what works for them now might change in the future, and care should be taken to ensure that students are not pigeonholed into one of the individual learning styles. A student may have identified **Visual** methods as their preferred choice, but this does not mean this is the *only* way they can learn, or that it is the only way they will be able to learn in the future.

Remember to use terminology that is consistent and accessible, so the terms **looking, listening** and **doing** might be simpler to understand than **Visual, Auditory** and **Kinaesthetic** depending on the different ability levels within the group.

Activity 3 Revision Practice

Students are asked to look in their folders and discuss the contents with each other. Each folder should also contain a handout with the stationery listed. Discuss how the different items might be used to revise, emphasising links between the method of revision and whether this links to one of the senses. Do index cards to **Make a Flashcard** involve **Visual** and **Kinaesthetic** approaches? Is moulding clay to **Make a Model** Kinaesthetic? Are **sticky notes** more **Visual**?

Here the facilitator might also want to refer to the revision brainstorm created in the last session so that previous methods listed can be matched to one or even two sensory channels discussed. Perhaps the students can label the previous week's responses with the letters **V (Visual), A (Auditory)** or **K (Kinaesthetic)** depending on where they think each strategy fits.

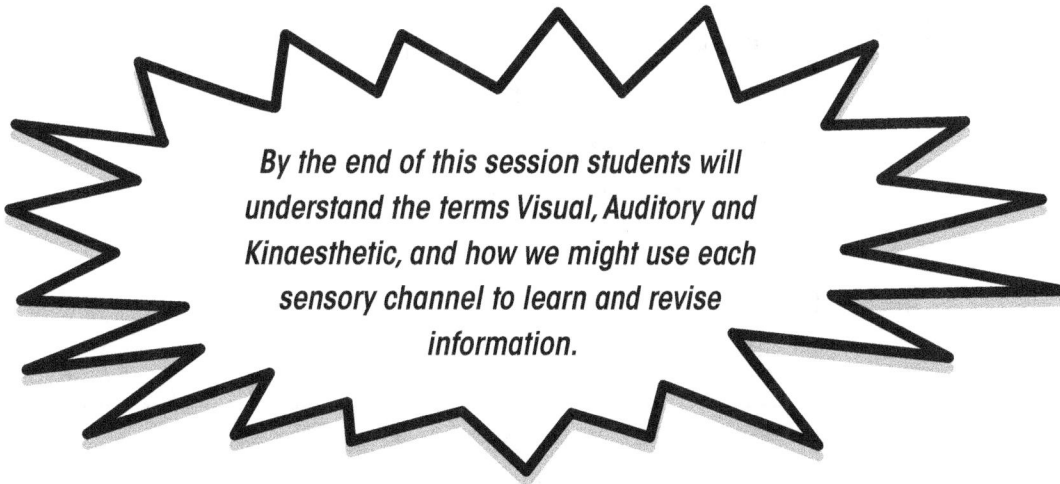

By the end of this session students will understand the terms Visual, Auditory and Kinaesthetic, and how we might use each sensory channel to learn and revise information.

Session 2

Session Plan 2   Warm-up Game p. 107 / Resources 2 pp. 55–57

Area of focus: Visual (Looking), Auditory (Listening), Kinaesthetic (Doing)		
Warm-up Game	Senses Bag – Pass the Object	
Activity	**Task**	**Materials/Resources needed**
1	**Study Skills Folder** Individual study skills folders are given out to each student. Items in the folder are discussed using the objects or the handout. Students can add to the images on the handout if they can think of other things that might help, e.g. a set of headphones.	A new pre-prepared folder filled with coloured pens/stickers/highlighters/sticky notes/moulding clay/set of flashcards, coloured paper. Study skills handout from the resource pack.
2	**How Do I Learn?** Students are given the survey and write V, A or K next to the one that they relate to the most. They then add up the numbers of V A K to see where they score the highest.	How Do I Learn survey. Pens for students to mark their answers V A K. Descriptions of what these three categories mean on a whiteboard.
3	**Revision Practice** Introduce Session 1 brainstorm where revision methods have already been discussed based on student contributions. Let the students think about which ones match their strengths, and whether they think they might try others now based on the V A K survey?	Revision brainstorm from previous week. Pens for students so they can go back to their ideas and mark them as V A K.
Follow-up Activity	Students personalise their study skills folders.	

Session 2

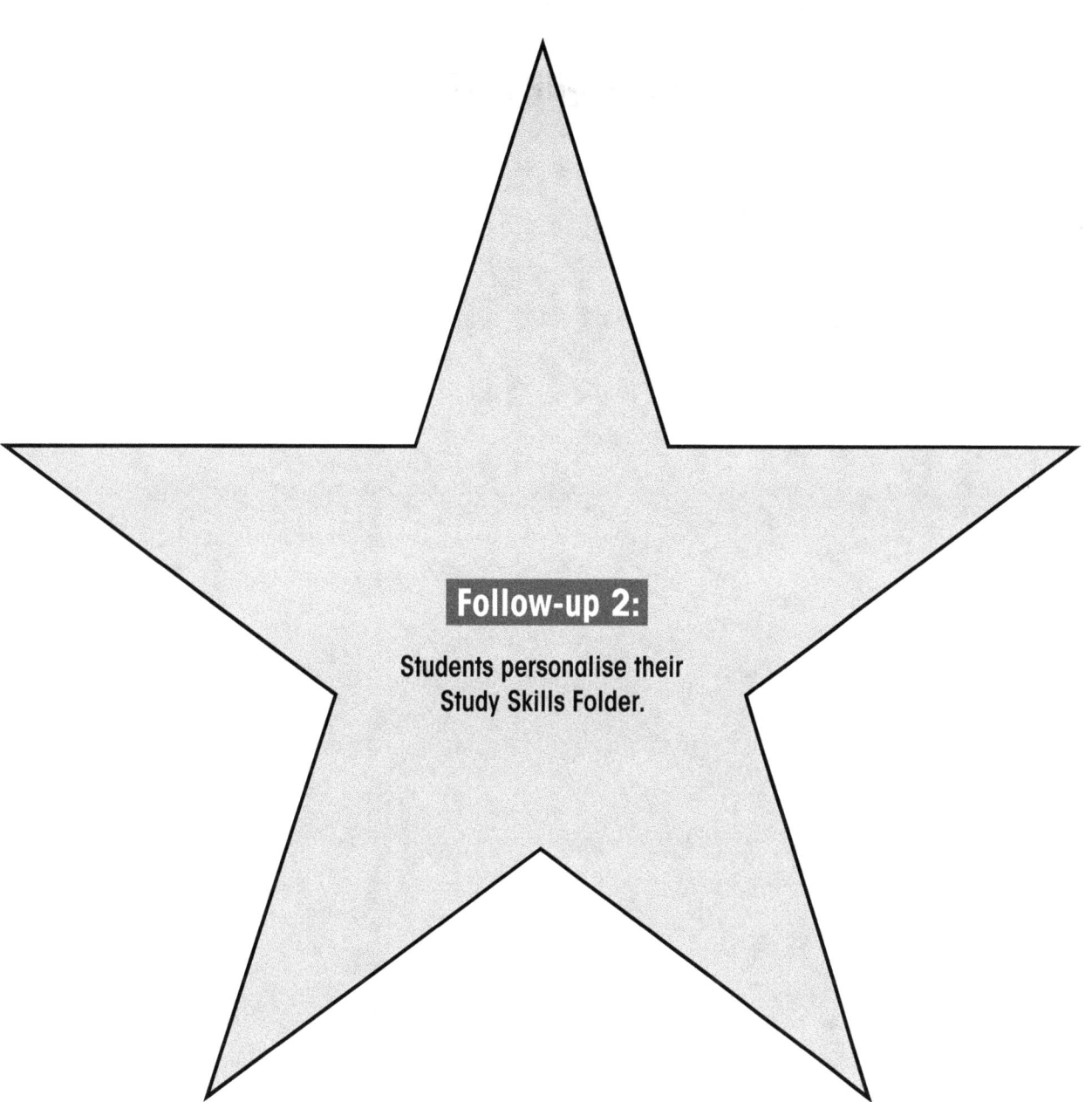

Follow-up 2:
Students personalise their Study Skills Folder.

Session 2

FOLLOW-UP 2 NOTES

Session 3
Focus: Visual (Looking)

The next three sessions will focus on the revision techniques that are assigned to each sensory channel.

Visual strategies are probably the ones that are most frequently used with SLCN students as they often struggle with using solely the auditory channel. Students who struggle with listening and auditory processing skills are much more likely to benefit from this method over others. Making a flashcard and a mind map are both revision methods which are tried and tested, suiting a range of individuals and not just those with SLCN.

Activity 1 Make a Flashcard

The facilitator talks through the instructions that have been provided with the resources. Producing a flashcard also creates opportunities to reinforce specific spatial or linguistic concepts that are potentially challenging such as:

Top/Middle/Bottom/Left/Right/Between/Both/Bold/Bright/Large/Small/Long/Short/Underline

Students with SLCN are much more likely to learn and retain complex linguistic concepts when taught functionally and related to events and activities that are meaningful to them. The examples of flashcards that are included with the resources can also be used to show examples although the facilitator could also use any pre-made cards.

Activity 2 Flashcard Competition

The students create their own flashcards. It is important to emphasise the need for writing to be BIG and BOLD, the colours to be BRIGHT and to make the information memorable. Encourage them to use pictures. A simple drawing might also be able to convey a message if it symbolises the word they are trying to learn. Images can be downloaded from the Internet or provided by the facilitator in advance if drawing is likely to be a challenge.

Session 3

Give praise for *all* efforts. The aim is to keep the images uncomplicated. The students need to understand that the flashcard does not have to contain lots of information, just one or two key points, and that making the keyword or idea stand out with use of colours, pictures and symbols will make their revision visually memorable. A sample of a flashcard is also included in the resources.

Activity 3 Make a Mind Map

The facilitator talks through the steps involved in creating a mind map this time, again using the instructions given in the resources. It is useful to think ahead of what this will include. Often a mind map works better if the information the student needs to remember is more than a list of keywords, e.g. thinking about an event in history, specific characters or themes inked to a narrative, or a broad science topic such as energy or digestion.

The mind map has a potential advantage over a flashcard as much more information can be added, interlinking a greater number of words, themes, concepts and ideas.

> *By the end of this session, the students will have had the opportunities to create a flashcard and a mind map, and to discuss other possible Visual methods of revision.*

Session 3

Session Plan 3   Warm-up Game p. 108 / Resources 3 pp. 58–65

Area of focus: Visual (Looking)		
Warm-up Game	**Spot the Difference**	
Activity	**Task**	**Materials/Resources needed**
1	**Make a Flashcard** The facilitator talks through how to make a flashcard and students follow the step-by-step instructions. The facilitator shows the students and example of a flashcard as they go through the instructions.	How to Make a Flashcard – instructions. Pre-made flashcard.
2	**Flashcard Competition** Students are asked to create their own flashcard in a competition. The prize is then awarded to the flashcard that covers most of the requirements set out in the instructions. It helps if there is an independent judge. The students can also "vote" themselves for the flashcard they think is the best depending on the size of the group.	A prize for the best flashcard! Index cards and coloured pens.
3	**Make a Mind Map** The instructions are given on how to make a mind map and the students make one as a group or in pairs based on a topic given. Doing one mind map as a group means that the facilitator can choose a topic that is relevant and ask each student to offer one fact they know about it. The facilitator can then lead this activity to ensure that the key features of a mind map are included and that every student's response is recorded in some way.	Large A2 or A3 sheet of paper. How to Make a Mind Map – instructions. Coloured pens.
Follow-up Activity	Visual methods handout given. Students use one Visual method to support their revision before the next session.	

Session 3

Follow-up 3:

Visual methods handout given.

Students must use one Visual method to support their revision.

FOLLOW-UP 3 NOTES

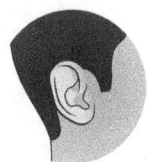

Session 4
Focus: Auditory (Listening)

This session focuses on listening and how the students might use auditory methods to remember key information. The three revision methods described here are how to **Make a Mnemonic** (linking initial letters of a word or list of words to another word or concept which is more memorable), **Record It**, so recording information onto a tablet or smartphone to hear it back, and **Discuss It**, where revision material can be discussed with a partner or in a group.

Students with SLCN can often have variable listening skills, so auditory methods may need to be reinforced with visual or kinaesthetic approaches to be fully effective. Research has also indicated that repetition and rehearsal strategies work best when they are supported with mental imagery and visualisation, so this should be encouraged whilst keeping the focus primarily on auditory input.

Activity 1 Make a Mnemonic

Students are introduced to the idea of a mnemonic by explaining that we can remember things by making a link between the first letter of words we need to learn to another word that might be more memorable. Linking can be to a letter, sound or an image. As this session is dedicated to sounds, the student is encouraged to think about how we can revise key words using the initial sounds. Some common mnemonics are included in the resources. Students attempt to create their own either using the example in the resources or one more pertinent to them at the time.

As mnemonic is a difficult word to say, the phrase "letters and words" might be an easier way to explain this approach.

Activity 2 Record It

This activity is simple and surprisingly motivating for many students once they have practised it. This will require a piece of sound recording equipment such as a smartphone or tablet. The facilitator thinks of a word that they must remember and asks each student to say the word

Session 4

into the recording device choosing a tone to say it in, e.g. they can say it loud, say it fast, say it slow, or the student can say it in a way that relates to its meaning. An example would be an adjective describing an emotion such as "astonished" could be said *using a high-pitched, surprised voice*, whereas "sombre" could be said *quietly, using a sad voice*. This is then played back after everybody the group has contributed.

As students become confident with this, they can be given opportunities to become more creative, e.g. they might want to "sing" or "rap" the word to make it more memorable.

Activity 3   Discuss It

Discussion should always be a key method for revising and is probably one of the most effective as students can inspire each other and learn at the same time. Discussion can be encouraged in a learning group, facilitated 1:1 with a parent or a teacher, on the telephone or through a video call. Discussion enables the group to vocalise and deepen their understanding of a subject. They may also be more able to remember the experience of having a discussion or debate about a subject over a piece of writing that they have read or written down.

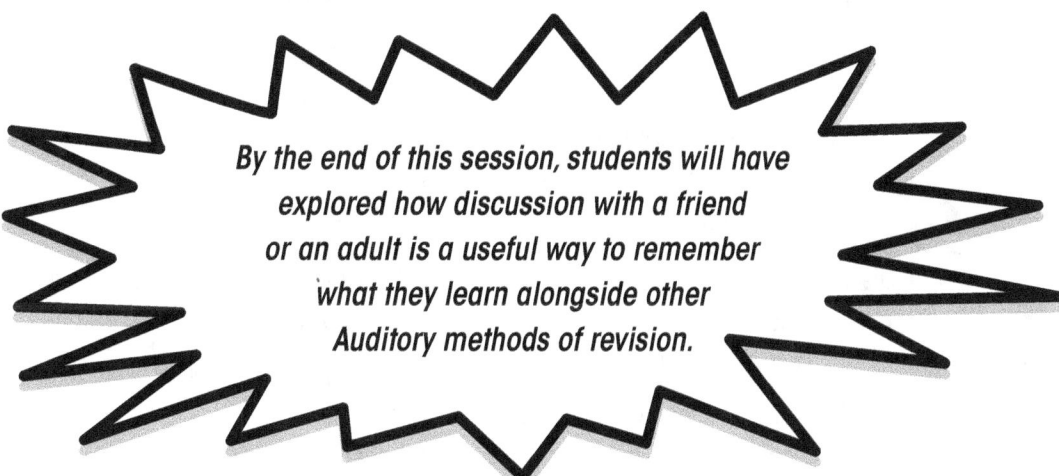

By the end of this session, students will have explored how discussion with a friend or an adult is a useful way to remember what they learn alongside other Auditory methods of revision.

Session 4

Session Plan 4
Warm-up Game p. 108 / Resources 4 pp. 66–70

Area of focus: Auditory (Listening)		
Warm-up Game	**Syllable Race**	
Activity	**Task**	**Materials/Resources needed**
1	**Make a Mnemonic** The facilitator introduces the idea of a mnemonic and talks about ones they might know using the examples given in the list. The key is how to make the sound of a word they need to learn memorable. The facilitator then gives them the letters linked to different alternative energies with the example on the handout. The students get into groups and try and think of their own.	**Make a Mnemonic** handout. Example of a mnemonic for learning different renewable energy.
2	**Record It** Students are given a keyword word or quote to record and playback. The students should be encouraged to experiment with different ways to say the word that might add meaning to it.	Smartphone/Tablet. Example of a word either from the list of curriculum words or another word that they need to learn for their exams.
3	**Discuss It** The group is shown an image relating to a topic to start a discussion. E.g. the theme of supernatural versus natural. Each student is prompted to add to the discussion, e.g. starting with a definition or example of something which is natural and something which is supernatural, so "nature and forests" are natural but "witches and ghosts" are supernatural.	A key theme or image relating to a topic they are studying. E.g. "supernatural versus natural" is a theme of *Macbeth*. So here you might want a picture of the witches to start off the discussion. "Wh?" prompts such as **Who? Where? When? What happens? Why?** to support discussion topics. The discussion could also be recorded on a recording device so that it can be accessed again at a later date. Alternatively it could be forwarded to the students to listen to again in their own time as part of their revision.
Follow-up Activity	Auditory methods handout is given. Students choose one Auditory revision method to practise at home.	

Session 4

Session 4

FOLLOW-UP 4 NOTES

Session 5
Focus: Kinaesthetic (Doing)

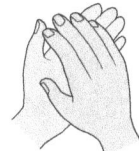

Kinaesthetic strategies to support revision are probably the least used of the three learning modalities as most traditional revision techniques will focus on visual or auditory methods. Using a kinaesthetic approach involves physical ways of learning, giving the individual student greater options in their "revision toolbox", thus increasing awareness of strategies that might work for them.

The kinaesthetic approach concerns adding movement and motion to everything you need to learn. A simple hand gesture could be used to help a student learn and remember a word. This could be linked to a known signed system or be completely new, e.g. a gesture that a student makes up to represent a word. For example, you could say the word "veil" and use your hands to make a physical hand gesture for covering your face with a veil. The gesture you make enables that word to instantly become memorable! Here three revision methods are used, **Make a Model, Walk and Talk** and **Sign It.**

Activity 1 Make a Model

Students are encouraged to express an idea or concept they need to revise for using their modelling clay. This activity is designed to support keyword learning in a kinaesthetic manner as students are asked to guess which words the others in the group have made.

Using modelling clay might also help some students with sensory processing difficulties to self-regulate and reach a point where they can be more ready to learn and take in information.

Activity 2 Walk and Talk

This technique applies to both visual and kinaesthetic methods. The method involves writing a word onto a sticky note and placing it on a piece of furniture in the classroom. The student reads the word (it could be a symbol or a picture with a word) as they go around the room, saying the word each time they pass the note.

Session 5

Eventually they should be able to recall all the words, simply by association with the piece of furniture. The "doing" method involves the movement as the student walks around the room. For the student who needs frequent breaks and movement this method is perfect!

Activity 3 Sign It

Using simple gestures and mime can support memory skills, particularly for students with SLCN for whom learning through just listening or looking alone is not always enough. For some students, signing is an invaluable method of supporting learning, and for revision it adds an extra multisensory prompt that can only be positive when trying to teach learners new words and, more importantly, a method of retaining a new word.

This activity works with the group split into pairs. Each pair is given a keyword from the curriculum words list and asked to mime it individually to their partner. The other student then needs to guess what that word is. This could alternatively be done with one person miming to the whole group.

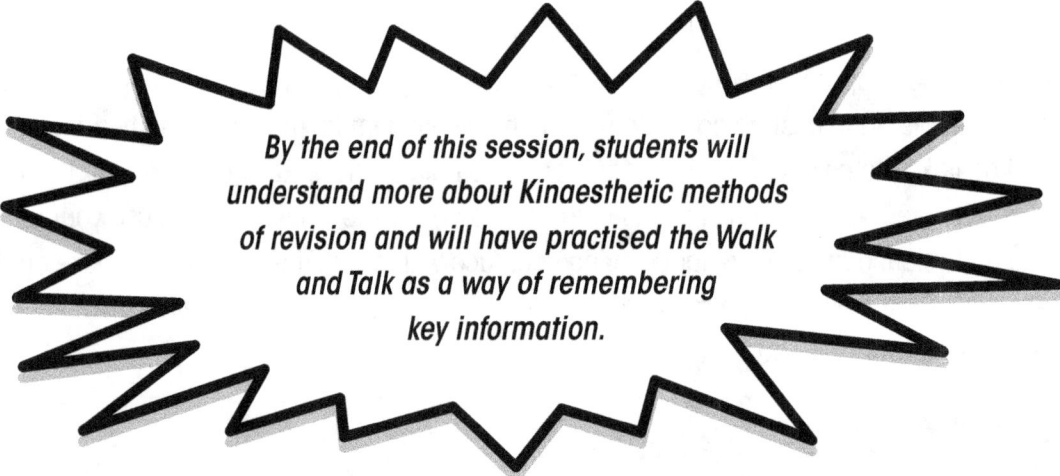

By the end of this session, students will understand more about Kinaesthetic methods of revision and will have practised the Walk and Talk as a way of remembering key information.

Session 5

Session Plan 5 — Warm-up Game p. 108 / Resources 5 pp. 71–80

Area of focus: Kinaesthetic (Doing)		
Warm-up Game	**Find the Shape**	
Activity	**Task**	**Materials/Resources needed**
1	**Make a Model** A word is given to individual students linked to a topic they might be learning. The students then try to make a model in clay to represent that word.	Modelling clay. A list of words (this can be taken from the curriculum words in the appendix or be ones linked to what they are learning).
2	**Walk and Talk** Words/pictures are placed onto sticky notes, and the notes are then placed on several pieces of furniture around the room. The student is asked to name the word given as they walk past it, paying attention to the word and saying it out loud, each time.	Sticky notes. A list of 6–8 keywords that they need to learn, taken from the curriculum list or from another list which they might need to learn for an upcoming exam.
3	**Sign It** Each student is given a word which they have to gesture or mime. The rest of the students in the group must guess what that word is. More formal signing methods could also be introduced here, such as BSL or Makaton. It is important to emphasise that the sign itself does not need to be perfect; it can be any hand gesture which is memorable.	List of words using curriculum words in the appendix or other ones which are relevant to their study.
Follow-up Activity	Kinaesthetic handout given. Student practises one Kinaesthetic approach to revision at home.	

Copyright material from Bhaveshi Kumar (2019), *Study Skills for Students with SLCN*, Routledge

Session 5

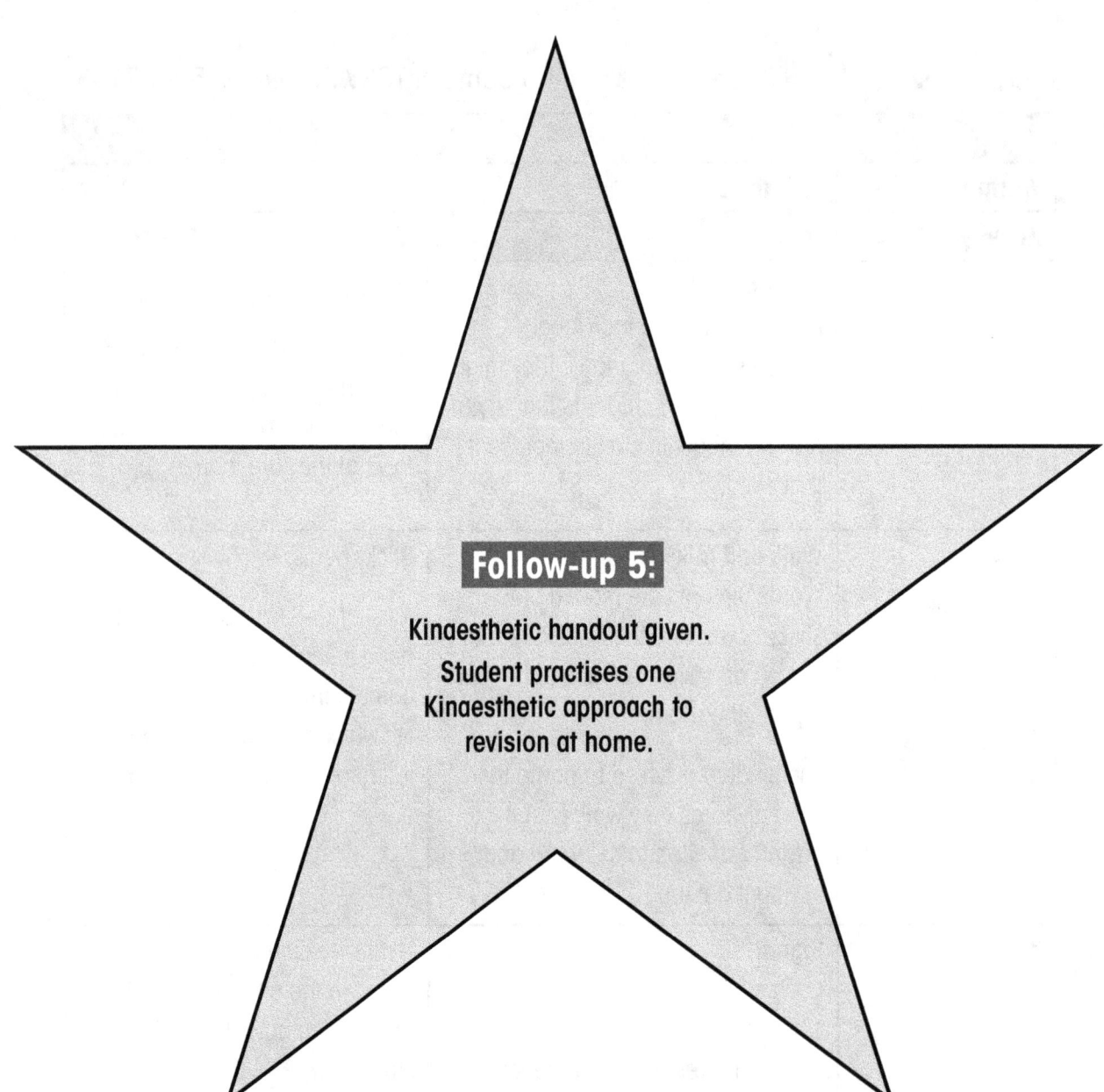

Follow-up 5:

Kinaesthetic handout given. Student practises one Kinaesthetic approach to revision at home.

Session 5

FOLLOW-UP 5 NOTES

Session 6

Focus: Time and Time Concepts

Students with SLCN struggle with organisation and planning. This session focuses on how the student might begin to plan their revision, including fun activities that allow them to think about time and time concepts. A revision timetable can help alleviate any stress the students have about their exams, which for those with SLCN is often linked to either not knowing what to expect or a lack of preparation.

Activity 1 The Time Game

This activity will help the student think about time concepts and apply these to everyday situations, by having to guess the length of time it takes to do certain familiar activities. This is a good way to introduce the concept of time in a fun way and something that can be adapted for different students depending on their levels of ability. The topic chosen can be anything that is interesting or relevant to them, e.g. how long their favourite film or sporting event might be.

This activity will allow students to understand more about time in relation to the time they will spend studying for or sitting an exam.

Activity 2 Make a Revision Timetable

Students are rarely given a specific revision or exam timetable in schools. Having a revision timetable helps students not only with organising and planning time but also with alleviating stress around knowing when exams begin and where exactly they take place. Focus should be made on why planning is important, e.g. it helps the student to feel more organised and prepared.

The timetable will also allow the student to include the other things they will need to do during the process of revising. Most importantly space should be made for fun, relaxation and downtime.

Session 6

Activity 3 — My Timeline

Students create their own personal timeline, outlining events that might have taken place previously such as when and where they went to their primary school, when they had their first pet or holidays. This is then linked to any future aspirations or plans they have. This will provide students with opportunities to share more personal experiences with the group and use time concepts in a way that is relevant to them.

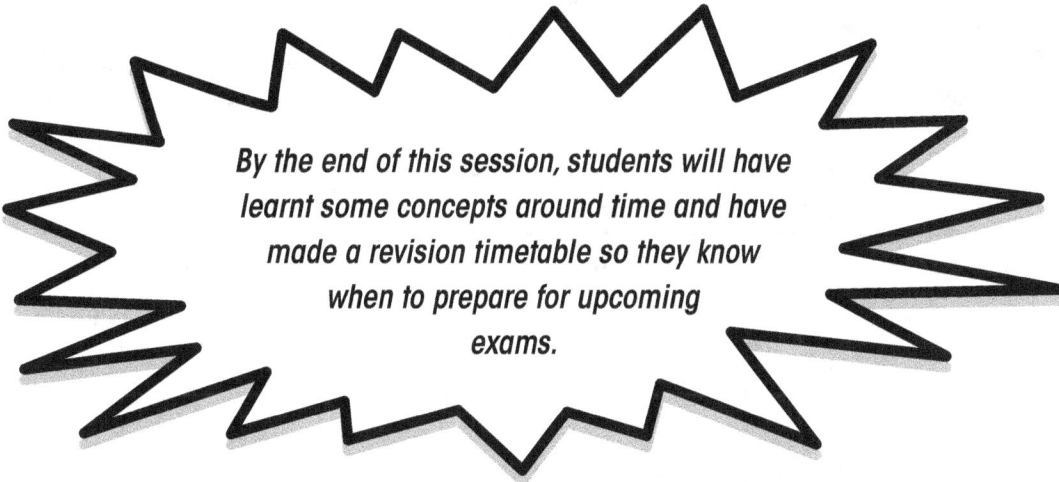

By the end of this session, students will have learnt some concepts around time and have made a revision timetable so they know when to prepare for upcoming exams.

Session 6

Session Plan 6 — Warm-up Game p. 108 / Resources 6 pp. 81–84

Area of focus: Time Concepts		
Warm-up Game	**Time Game – Categories**	
Activity	**Task**	**Materials/Resources needed**
1	**The Time Game** Concepts linked to time are introduced. Can the students guess how long some activities take? The students are asked to guess how long certain things take either individually or in small groups.	The Time Game. An analogue clock to refer to. A prize for the winner of the time game. (Students get marks for being the closest as the exact times are not needed!)
2	**Make a Revision Timetable** The facilitator introduces the revision timetable, asking the students to think about times of the day when they might be able to revise. This also gives them an opportunity to talk about times that are difficult e.g. because they are swimming, have a personal tutor, play football. This also gives the students an opportunity to share their interests with other members of the group. The students are asked to plot one 30-minute slot in the week for homework/revision and others for breaks, rest and rewards.	Revision Timetable. A visual calendar with dates for exams if this is available so that this can be recorded somewhere onto their timetables.
3	**My Timeline** Timelines: What will I be doing in the future? Students can use the template to help them write their own timeline. This helps students think about time in the wider sense bringing in concepts such as Now / Before / After.	My Timeline sheet or big A3 sheet of paper to which all students can contribute.
Follow-up Activity	Students take their revision timetables home and place them somewhere they can see them regularly. Students try and plan 30 minutes of revision/study time over the week or weekend.	

Session 6

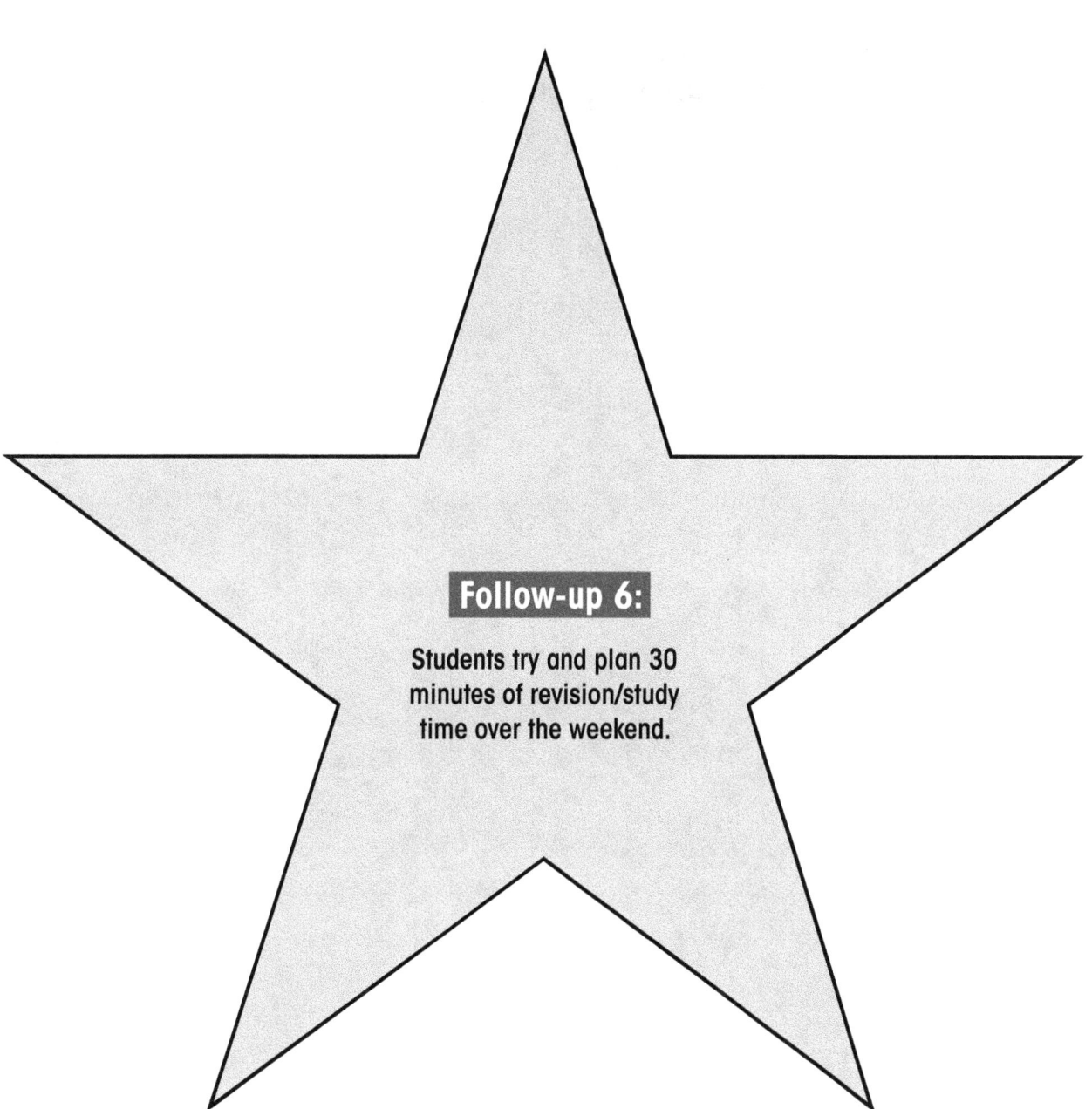

Session 6

FOLLOW-UP 6 NOTES

Session 7

Focus: Exams and Command Words – Complex Vocabulary

The term "command words" refers to language specifically used in exam questions. This vocabulary can often be a challenge for many SLCN students and misunderstanding a word like "summarise" or "argue" can be costly in exam conditions, causing the student to lose marks through not responding to the exact directive. Students will often make the mistake of writing everything they know into an exam paper rather than responding to the specifics of the question, so it is important that these words and their context are understood.

The focus of this week's session is to learn exam words and look at how SLCN students can be supported with the task of learning complicated vocabulary that is often used at secondary level, including words with multiple meanings.

Activity 1 Exam Words (Command Words)

Students play a match-up activity with the exam word and its description. This gives the student an opportunity to be taught any new exam words they have not come across before and discuss any subtle differences in command word vocabulary that they encounter.

Activity 2 Exam Words (Command Words): Word Search

Students work in pairs to activate what they have already learnt about exam words. This allows any new vocabulary to be revisited that enables them to further retain their meaning.

The key to learning vocabulary is to try and incorporate it into as many learning tasks as possible, so that their acquisition of those words is generalised.

Session 7

Activity 3 — Multiple Meanings

Students are given a range of curriculum words with multiple meanings; these cards could be cut out and made into a simple track game or be shared as cards amongst the group. Each student must identify more than one meaning for the word, e.g. "source" "sounds like **sauce** you have on your hot dog but it can also be **evidence** found in history books relating to a person, time or event".

The activity could be adapted so that more basic vocabulary is used for students needing a more differentiated activity.

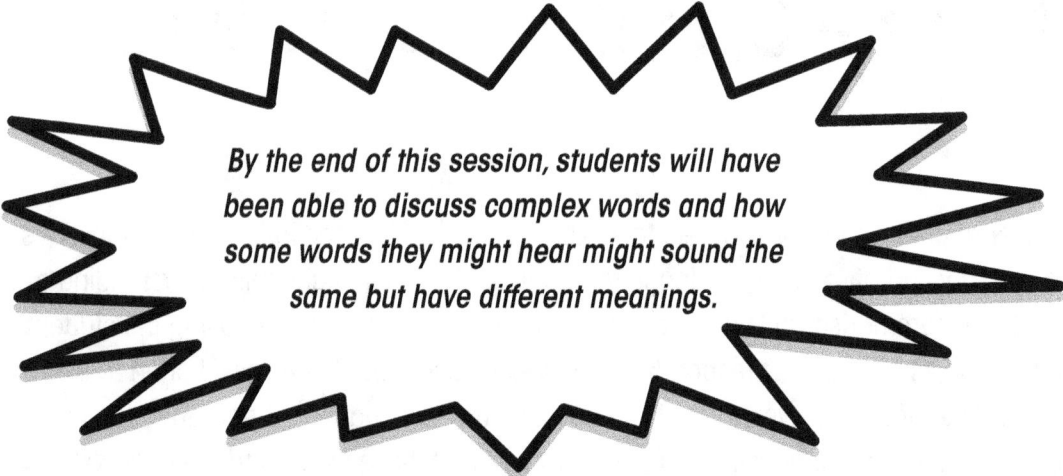

By the end of this session, students will have been able to discuss complex words and how some words they might hear might sound the same but have different meanings.

Session Plan 7

Session 7

Warm-up Game p. 109 / Resources 7 pp. 85–90

Area of Focus: Exams and Command Words – Complex Vocabulary		
Warm-up Game	**Word Definition Game**	
Activity	**Task**	**Materials/Resources needed**
1 *Summarise Argue Evaluate*	**Exam Words** The student is introduced to command words and their definitions. The students are first encouraged to give you a definition of what they think it means before the words and definitions are placed in front of them.	Use cards for Exam Words in matching game with the command word and definition cut out in separate piles. Students must match up the correct card with the definition.
2	**Exam Words: Word Search** Each student completes the command words word search. The aim of this game is to help reinforce and embed some of the meanings of any new words they may have learnt in Activity 1. The facilitator should also use this opportunity to talk about how these words are used in exams and why it is important that the students learn them.	Word Search activity. Pens.
3 *Meanings?*	**Multiple Meanings** Multiple and double meanings words are given out. The students can do this individually or in pairs, or this would work as a team game, with each side giving as many definitions as they can for each word.	Cards are given out and the students are asked to think about the words and double meanings.
Follow-up Activity	Students take out their study skills folder and choose any of the revision methods to remember one of the new words learnt in this session.	

Session 7

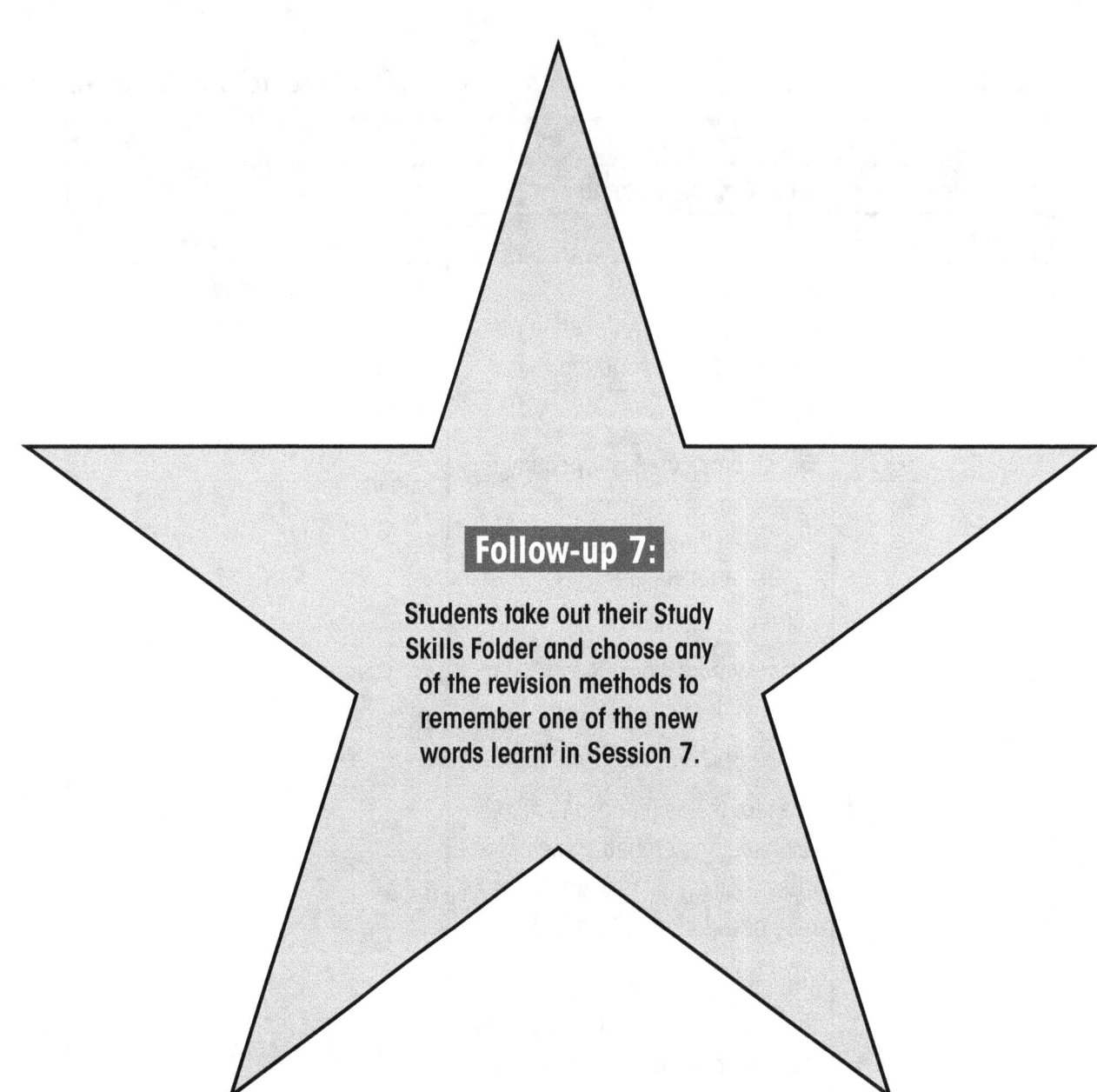

Follow-up 7:

Students take out their Study Skills Folder and choose any of the revision methods to remember one of the new words learnt in Session 7.

Session 7

FOLLOW-UP 7 NOTES

Session 8

Focus: Beat Exam Stress

Exam situations can be overwhelming and often therefore a cause of stress. Students with SLCN may struggle as much with the exam environment as with the examination paper itself. The sensory overload, unfamiliar surroundings combined with the necessity to sit still in silence for the duration of the exam can be a challenge for many students.

This session aims to provide the student with information to deal with these adverse situations and the opportunity to discuss any access arrangements that they may have. Access arrangements could be having a reader or a scribe, having extra time, being able to use a laptop. These arrangements are usually granted through the SEN department or local authority and focus on aspects of the examination process individual students may find difficult. This session also looks at ways stress can be managed using calming strategies, positive affirmations and mindfulness.

Activity 1 The Exam and Access Arrangements

There are often certain things which students with SLCN are unaware of when it comes to exams, e.g. where and when the exam is taking place and the equipment they may need. Can they take highlighters into exams? Can they use a calculator? Are there access arrangements in place? Will they have a reader, scribe, extra time?

Where there are no arrangements in place, the students would still benefit from exploring the timings of exams and being able to answer an exam question in the time allocated.

Activity 2 Being Positive

In this activity the students are given a list of statements that they transform from a negative into a positive statement so a student might turn a statement like *"I wish I had more friends"* to *"I really like the friends I have and they really care about me"* The students can do this alone or with a partner.

Session 8

It is reported that the average person creates more negative thoughts in a day than positive ones. Students with SLCN can often suffer from extreme anxiety and stress that can exacerbate this situation, particularly as their overall coping mechanisms may be limited, leading on to negative thinking patterns and low self-esteem. The idea of positive thinking and having a "can do" approach links to the idea of encouraging students to become more confident and in better control when these negative thought patterns emerge.

Students also need to be reminded here that:

1) There is no such thing as **perfect** and

2) Getting high grades is **not** as important as them trying their best.

The more confident the student feels the more likely it is they will learn and remember information.

Activity 3 Mindfulness

The mindfulness approach is a method that enables students to relax and increase their ability to focus on the present. It is reported that students with SLCN are more likely to benefit from activities that encourage mindfulness than other neurotypical students because they are often more susceptible to difficulties with attention, sensory overload and anxiety. This exercise will enable the student to be introduced to mindfulness practice, where the facilitator is able to lead.

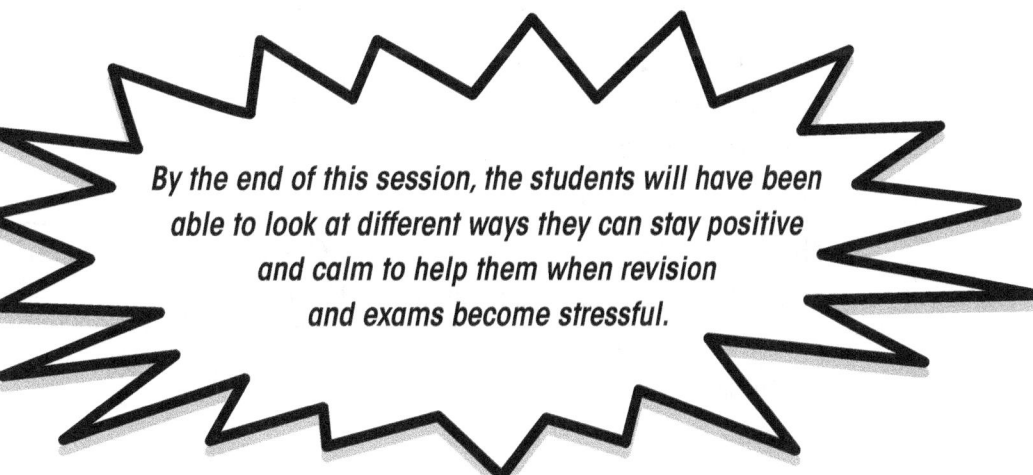

By the end of this session, the students will have been able to look at different ways they can stay positive and calm to help them when revision and exams become stressful.

Session 8

Session Plan 8 Warm-up Game p. 109 / Resources 8 pp. 91–94

Area of Focus: Beat Exam Stress		
Warm-up Game	**Music**	
Activity	**Task**	**Materials/Resources needed**
1	**Access Arrangements** There may be some students who do not have access arrangements. Here the facilitator can talk about the exam conditions and what they can expect; and more importantly what they can or cannot do in an exam setting and what they are allowed to use. E.g. can they have a calculator or a highlighter, and can they ask for a break?	Access arrangements should be investigated for each student before this session has begun. A list is then put up on the board so that each student understands what this means and how it will help them in an exam.
2	**Being Positive** Students are given written/verbal statements which are negative. They must try to convert those negative statements into positive statements. The students can try and think of something of their own to share with the group; the others can then volunteer an alternative to that student's statement.	List of positive statements sheet. Cut out the negative statements from the negative and positive beliefs handout. Give each pupil a self-limiting belief and see if they can turn it into something positive.
3	**Mindfulness** Each student is given an orange. The facilitator then begins the mindfulness meditation, speaking slowly to make sure that every student can participate. After the meditation the students share their experiences.	One orange for each pupil. Mindfulness meditation example which could be read out with the group or pre-recorded.
Follow-up Activity	Students practise one activity at home that makes them feel happy and relaxed, and report back the following session.	

Session 8

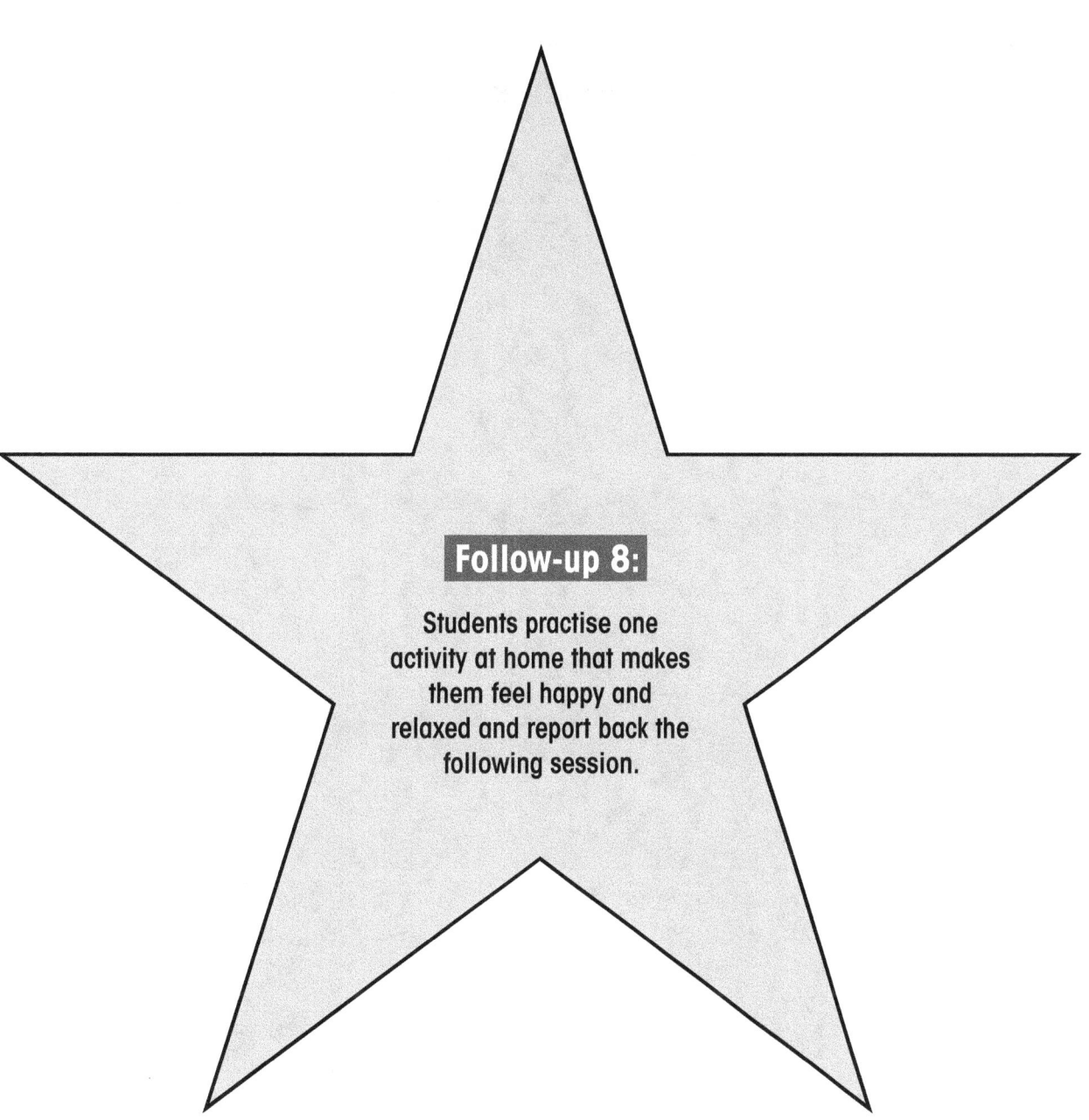

Follow-up 8:

Students practise one activity at home that makes them feel happy and relaxed and report back the following session.

Session 8

FOLLOW-UP 8 NOTES

Session 9
Focus: Be Healthy

Maintaining a healthy mind and a healthy body needs to be considered when discussing optimum conditions for revision and study. A healthy body can be achieved through diet, sleep and exercise. Healthy minds can, however, be much harder to define. Students are therefore given an opportunity to think about both and choose habits that they feel will enhance their studying process.

Food and diet regulate energy and mood. Certain foods have also been proven to support memory and cognitive function. Students are encouraged to have fun here by planning a recipe that incorporates at least one of these brain-boosting foods, e.g. making a smoothie or a salad.

Activity 1 Healthy Habits Game

The facilitator has objects in a large bag that are given out in turn. The students each pick out an object and identify the object and say why they think it is linked to being "healthy". As this is a game, the students should be allowed to think about each object for themselves and question its use. *What does a pillow represent? Sleep. Why is sleep healthy? Because sleep will help us not be tired at school and sleep can improve our memories.*

Objects in the bag could include:

- Dark chocolate (a piece of dark chocolate) – known to increase memory
- A pillow (to represent sleep) – which helps us be alert for exams and helps with memory
- A skipping rope (to represent exercise) – so our brains become active and we are alert
- Water (a bottle of water) – so we are hydrated
- Lavender – to promote sleep and relaxation
- Rosemary – known to increase alertness in small quantities

Session 9

- ◆ Classical music on headphones – to help calm the mind and focus
- ◆ Avocado – a superfood known to improve memory

Each student then picks one of the objects from the list which they think represents a good habit. This allows them to have a physical prompt to help them remember a healthy habit they might wish to pursue. Students can also offer their own ideas here, e.g. walking instead of getting the bus, having more breaks, including fish in their diets or anything else that they think they might need to improve mental and physical health.

Activity 2 Healthy Habits Poster

As different healthy habits are discussed, students are encouraged to produce a poster that they can put up in the classroom as a reminder. The poster will allow them to work together and be creative as they think of how they can maximise their chances of learning through taking better care of themselves, which will support the right state for learning, both at home and at school.

Activity 3 Feed Your Brain

The facilitator introduces food items that can go into the student's salad or smoothie. Students make a smoothie or a salad based on healthy ingredients that are suggested to improve memory and concentration. This task allows them to be practical and demonstrates another aspect of how a healthy mind and body are needed to enable them to perform at their best when trying to revise and study.

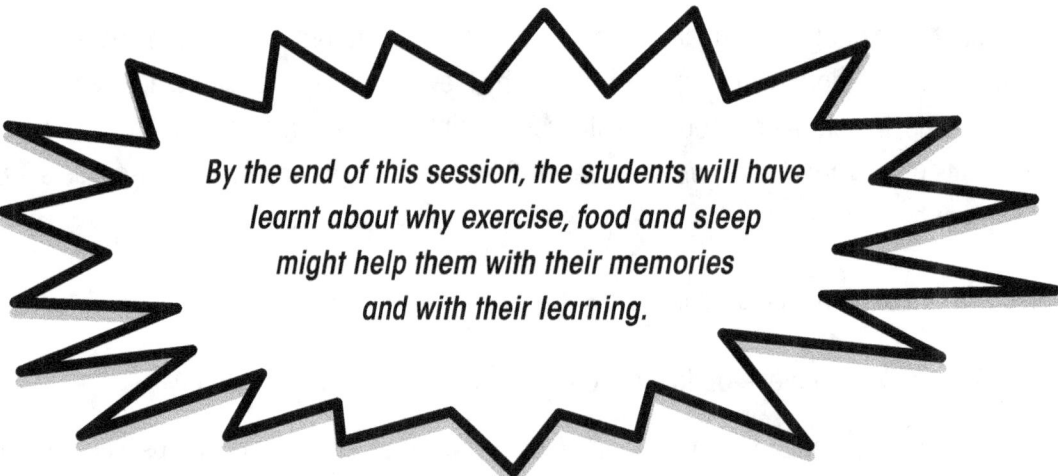

By the end of this session, the students will have learnt about why exercise, food and sleep might help them with their memories and with their learning.

Session 9

Session Plan 9   Warm-up Game p. 109 / Resources 9 pp. 95–97

Area of Focus: Be Healthy		
Warm-up Game	**Paper Plates**	
Activity	**Task**	**Materials/Resources needed**
1	**Healthy Habits Game** Different foods and objects are passed around. Students name the object and must tell you the link it has to being healthy. If the student guesses why the item is healthy, they put the item next to them. The winner is then the person who guesses the most healthy associations.	Avocado/Spinach/Rosemary/A pillow/A screen on a tablet which is OFF/Dark chocolate. The facilitator can add other things too e.g. a watch, a skipping rope.
2	**Healthy Habits Poster** Make a poster.	A3 sheet of paper. Coloured pens. Their poster can go up on the wall at school.
3	**Feed Your Brain** Students create a smoothie or salad using ingredients that "boost" brain power.	A blender. Smoothie/salad recipes. Essential ingredients. Access to a kitchen and support for cutting fruit or vegetables. or A3 page with pictures of healthy foods to make a collage of a smoothie or salad.
Follow-up Activity	Student chooses one target they want to achieve to support their study skills, e.g. regular bedtime, drink more water or do more exercise.	

Session 9

Follow-up 9:

Student chooses one target they want to achieve to support their study skills, e.g. regular bedtime, drink more water or do more exercise.

Session 9

FOLLOW-UP 9 NOTES

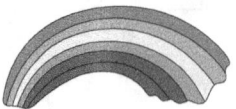

Session 10

Focus: Evaluation and Moving Forward

This session allows the student to evaluate their progress with revision and study skills with a personal plan that shows the measure of the progress they have made in the group. The final session is about reinforcing the students' own perceptions of their strengths referring to ideas at the start about what success might mean to them.

Every student has the potential to do well in school and different students offer different strengths. Students can be encouraged to think about famous icons, either now or in history, who may have struggled with personal challenges but went on to be successful.

Activity 1 V A K Recap

Students recap on what they have learned about the different methods of revision. Provide the students with the three headings, **Visual**, **Auditory** and **Kinaesthetic**, and ask the students what revision method they remember for each style of learning. The revision methods in the resources pack can be used as a sorting exercise, with students asked to assign each revision method to a sensory channel.

Activity 2 Student Evaluation: My Personal Plan

This an opportunity to gauge how far the students have progressed using the personal evaluation sheets.

The facilitator gives out the template for discussion, which can be discussed as a group or individually with each student. This can then be copied as a record of the individual's progress and shared with parents and teachers.

Session 10

Activity 3 "Believe Everything Is Possible"

Different photographs are given out and students look at the characteristics of certain people who have achieved success despite their perceived disability or having been given a label. Here the facilitator can prompt for:

Who were they? What did they achieve? What challenges did they face?

Did they have a diagnosis or label that we know about?

More able students may wish to discuss some of the "labels" they might have been given and what they understand about those labels. For example, do they understand the definitions of autism (ASD) or developmental language disorder (DLD) and what do they know about people who live with this? Students with autism are good at learning facts, students with DLD work better with visuals…do they agree with these statements? Can they relate these to themselves?

This is an opportunity for students to think again about their individual strengths and what makes them unique.

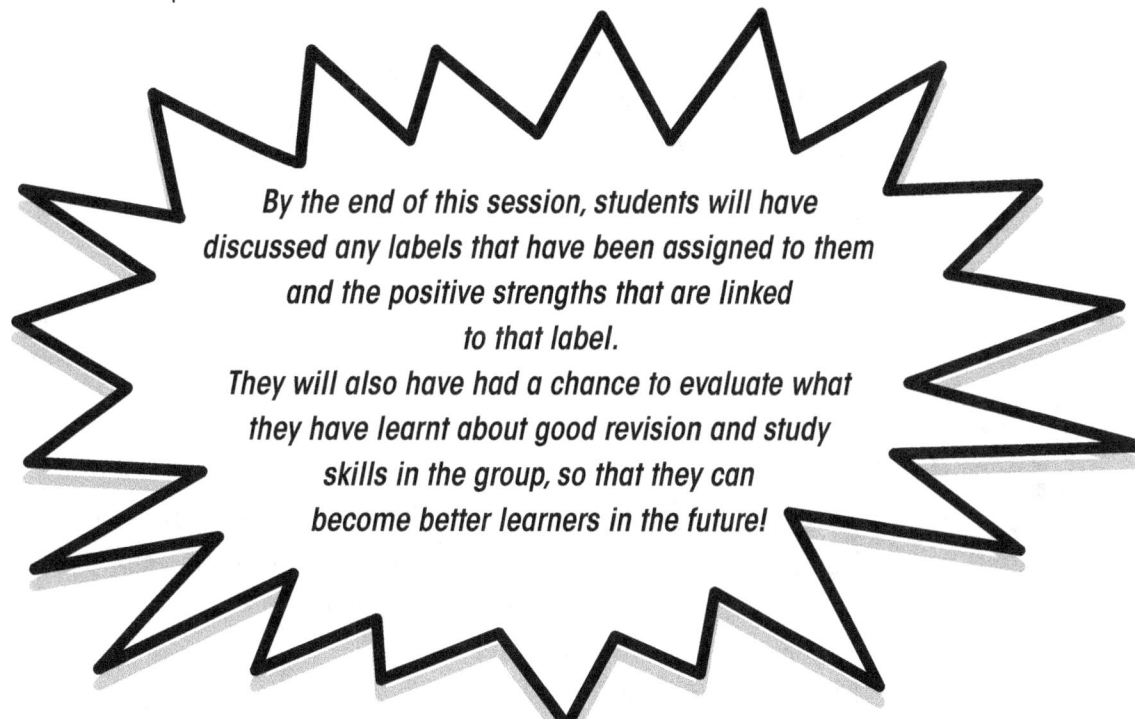

By the end of this session, students will have discussed any labels that have been assigned to them and the positive strengths that are linked to that label.
They will also have had a chance to evaluate what they have learnt about good revision and study skills in the group, so that they can become better learners in the future!

Session 10

Session Plan 10 Warm-up Game p. 110 / Resources 10 pp. 98–104

Area of Focus: Evaluation and Moving Forward		
Warm-up Game	**Compliments Game**	
Activity	**Task**	**Materials/Resources needed**
1	**V A K Recap** Students name as many revision methods as they can, corresponding to the three senses Visual, Auditory and Kinaesthetic.	Use the headings: **Visual (Looking), Auditory (Listening)** and **Kinaesthetic (Doing).** Three sets of revision cards for V, A and K.
2	**My Personal Plan** Each student fills out their plan and revisits their baseline from the start of the group.	My Personal Plan sheet. Pens.
3	**"Believe Everything Is Possible"** Students discuss famous people who have known disabilities who may have overcome challenges. The idea of having a label is discussed. Students can discuss any labels that may have been assigned to them and look through the My Label and Me advice sheets to see if they agree with the profiles.	Make a list of famous celebrities/historical figures who have known disabilities. Icons could include David Beckham (dyslexia), Albert Einstein (autism), Justin Timberlake (ADHD) or others who may have overcome other personal or physical challenges to achieve success. My Label and Me advice sheets.
Follow-up Activity	Students fill out their personal plans and share this with someone at home. One copy is kept in their study skills folders.	

Session 10

Follow-up 10:

Students to complete their Personal Plans and share this with someone in their family.

Students to keep a copy of their plan in their Study Skills Folders.

Session 10

FOLLOW-UP 10 NOTES

Session Plan Resources

Session Plan 1 Resources 52
Activity 1 Student Baseline Assessment 52
Activity 2 Why Study? 54

Session Plan 2 Resources 55
Activity 1 Study Skills Folder 55
Activity 2 How Do I Learn? 56

Session Plan 3 Resources 58
Activity 1 Make a Flashcard – instructions
             and example 58
Activity 3 Make a Mind Map – instructions
             and example 60
Revision Method Cards – Visual 63

Session Plan 4 Resources 66
Activity 1 Make a Mnemonic 66
Revision Method Cards – Auditory 68

Session Plan 5 Resources 71
Activity 1   Vocabulary Words 71
   (The words in the Resources are
   examples of vocabulary that can be
   used for Sessions 3, 4 and 5. However,
   you may wish to use your own!)
Revision Method Cards – Kinaesthetic 78

Session Plan 6 Resources 81
Activity 1 The Time Game 81
Activity 2 Make a Revision Timetable 82
Activity 3 My Timeline – example
             and template 83

Session Plan 7 Resources 85
Activity 1 Exam Words (Command Words) 85
Activity 2 Exam Words (Command Words):
             Word Search 87
Activity 3 Multiple Meanings 89

Session Plan 8 Resources 91
Activity 2 Being Positive 91
Activity 3 Mindfulness 93

Session Plan 9 Resources 95
Activity 2 Ideas for Healthy Habits Poster 95
Activity 3 Feed Your Brain 96

Session Plan 10 Resources 98
Activity 1 V A K Recap ....
   Use V A K Revision Method Cards from
   Sessions 3, 4 and 5
Activity 2 My Personal Plan 98
Activity 3 My Label and Me Advice Sheets:
             Autism, DLD, Dyspraxia, Dyslexia,
             ADHD 99

Student Baseline Assessment

Student Baseline Assessment

Name: ………………………………

Date: ………………………………

1. What is revision? _____

   _____

2. What are study skills? _____

   _____

3. I know how to revise for exams

   1--10

   ☹   ☺

4. At school if I need help with my schoolwork, I can ask

   _____

   _____

5. At home if I need help with my homework, I can ask

   _____

   _____

Student Baseline Assessment

6. The place I usually do my homework/revise is

   _____

   _____

7. If I don't understand a new word, I can

   _____

   _____

8. When I leave school, I want to

   _____

   _____

Why Study?

Studying and learning are important for ME because:

The facilitator to cut the statements out and place them in front of the students so they can organise them into preference.

| I want to get a good job  |

| I want my family to be proud  |

| I want to remember what I learn 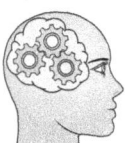 |

| I want to go to college  |

| I want to make my teachers happy  |

| I want to try my best  |

| Because learning is fun  |

My Study Skills Folder

Name:_____

_____

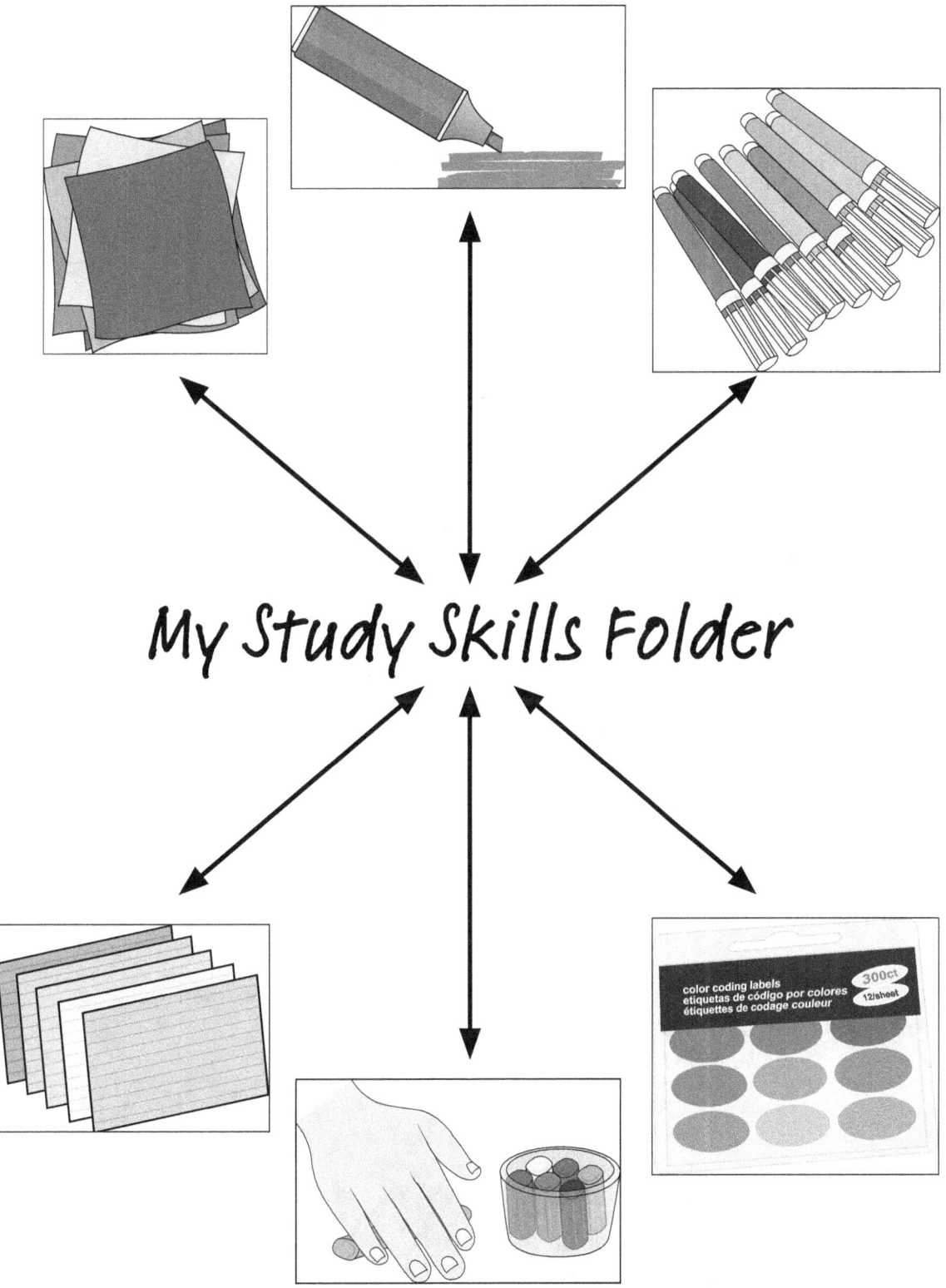

How Do I Learn?

Circle the ones which are like you!

1
I like lessons where we discuss things A
I like lessons where they show a film to watch V
I like lessons where we can move around or do a practical task like a science experiment K

2
It helps me learn when I see pictures to help me follow instructions V
It helps me learn when someone explains how to do it with me, talking slowly A
It helps me learn when someone shows me how to do it K

3
I like listening to stories on podcast or on a radio A
I like to read stories with pictures, I like comics V
I like acting and pretending to be characters in a story K

4
My favourite job would be on radio or a YouTuber A
My favourite job would be a car mechanic or gardener K
My favourite job would be an artist or designer V

5
In my spare time I like to do exercise or be outdoors in nature K
In my spare time I watch YouTube and play video games V
In my spare time I listen to music or the radio A

6
My best subject is PE K
My favourite subject is Music A
My favourite subject is Art V

7
I am good at learning physical skills K
I am good at learning people's names A
I am good at remembering people's faces V

How Do I Learn?

8

I am good at finding my way around school and finding my class if I go there a few times K

I am good at finding my way to my class if someone tells me where I need to go A

I am good at finding my way to class if I am given a map V

Students add up the number of V, A and K

V =   A =   K =

Which one are you?

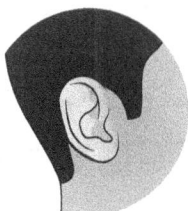

Mostly V: I prefer Visual. This means that I learn better when I can read something, or have pictures or videos to help me.

Mostly A: I prefer Auditory. This means that I learn better when I am listening to what others are saying, or when I say things over and over again until I remember it.

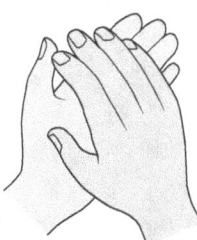

Mostly K: I prefer Kinaesthetic. This means that I learn better when I am active. I like to build or make things and I don't like to be still for too long.

Make a Flashcard

Make a Flashcard

Use BOTH sides of the card

Write the keyword in the MIDDLE of the card

Make the word BIG

Make the word STAND OUT – Draw a BORDER

Use DIFFERENT colours

Make it BRIGHT

Draw PICTURES or CUT PICTURES from a magazine and stick them on the card

Write a SHORT definition on the back of the card

Just write one or two sentences

Example Flashcard

Front of Flashcard

Heir

Back of Flashcard

Make a Mind Map

Take a BLANK PIECE OF PAPER

Start from the MIDDLE of the page

Draw PICTURE OR USE A WORD that shows the MAIN POINT of the map

Draw a CIRCLE around it

Draw a line OUT FROM THE CIRCLE

At the end of that line, DRAW A PICTURE or WRITE A KEYWORD to show your first point

CIRCLE this

To add MORE information, draw NEW LINES out

Go back to the MIDDLE then draw ANOTHER LINE OUT to make your SECOND point

Your map should look like spreading branches or roots of a tree

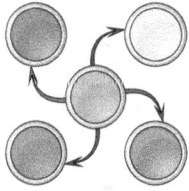

Remember:
- Use pictures or symbols
- Use A DIFFERENT colour for different branches, ideas or links
- Anything that stands out on the page will stand out in your mind
- Be creative

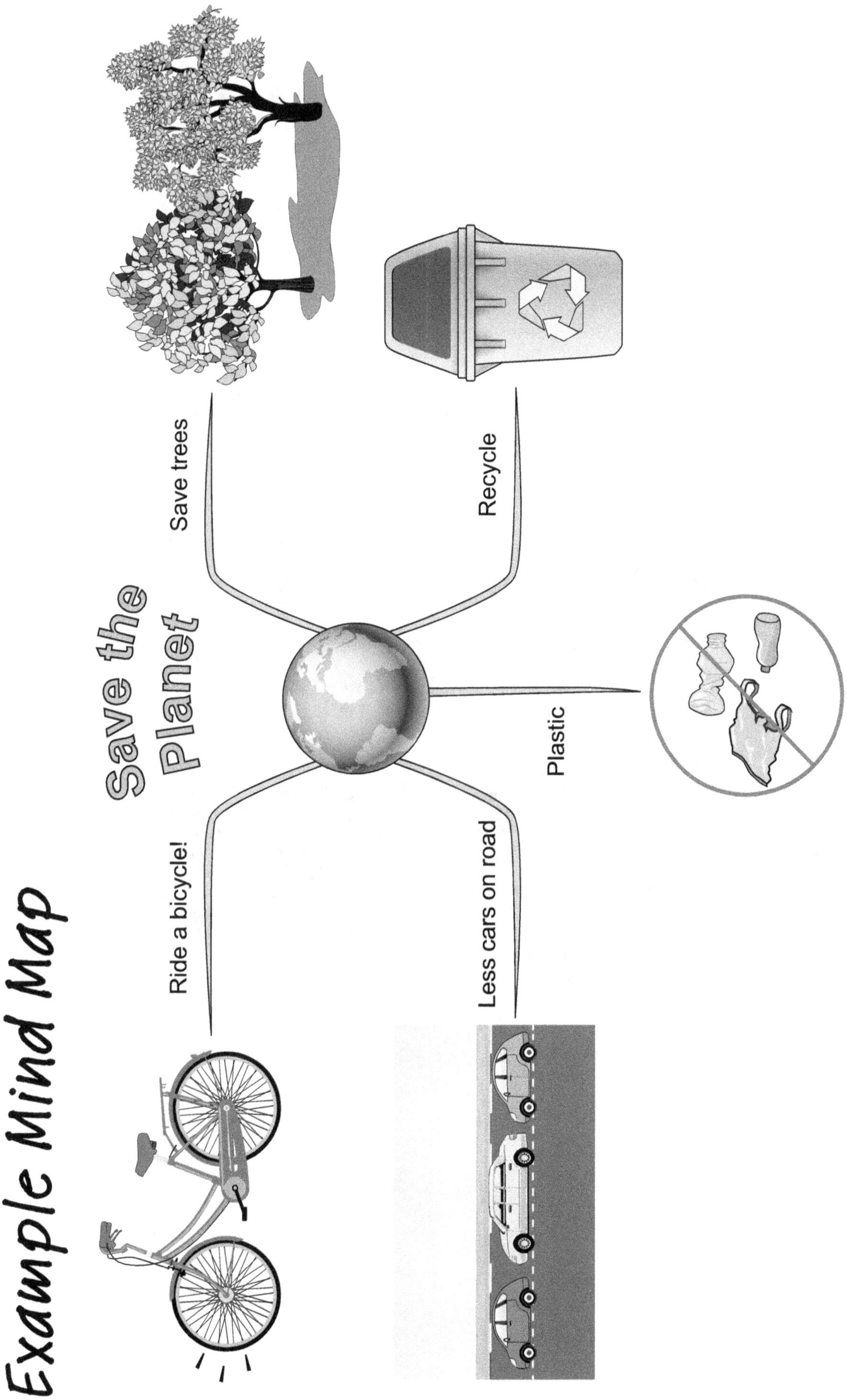

Example Mind Map

Example Mind Map

- Save trees
- Recycle
- Plastic
- Less cars on road
- Ride a bicycle!

Save the Planet

Visual (Looking)

Revision Cards – Visual

(Looking) methods

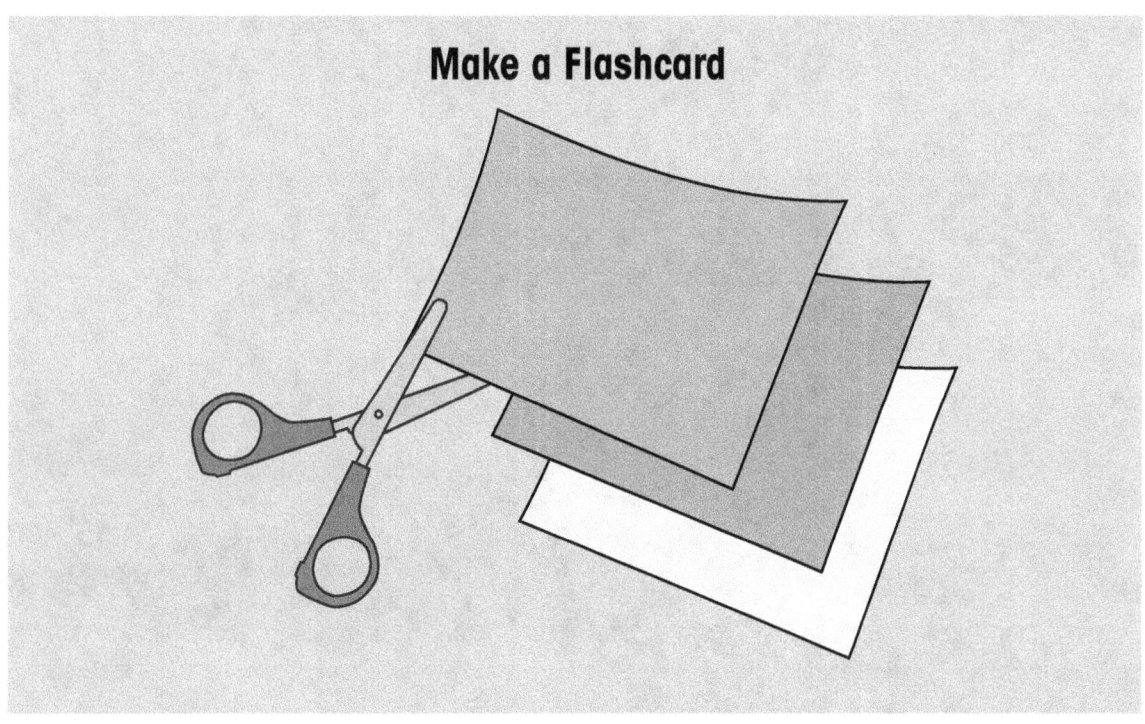

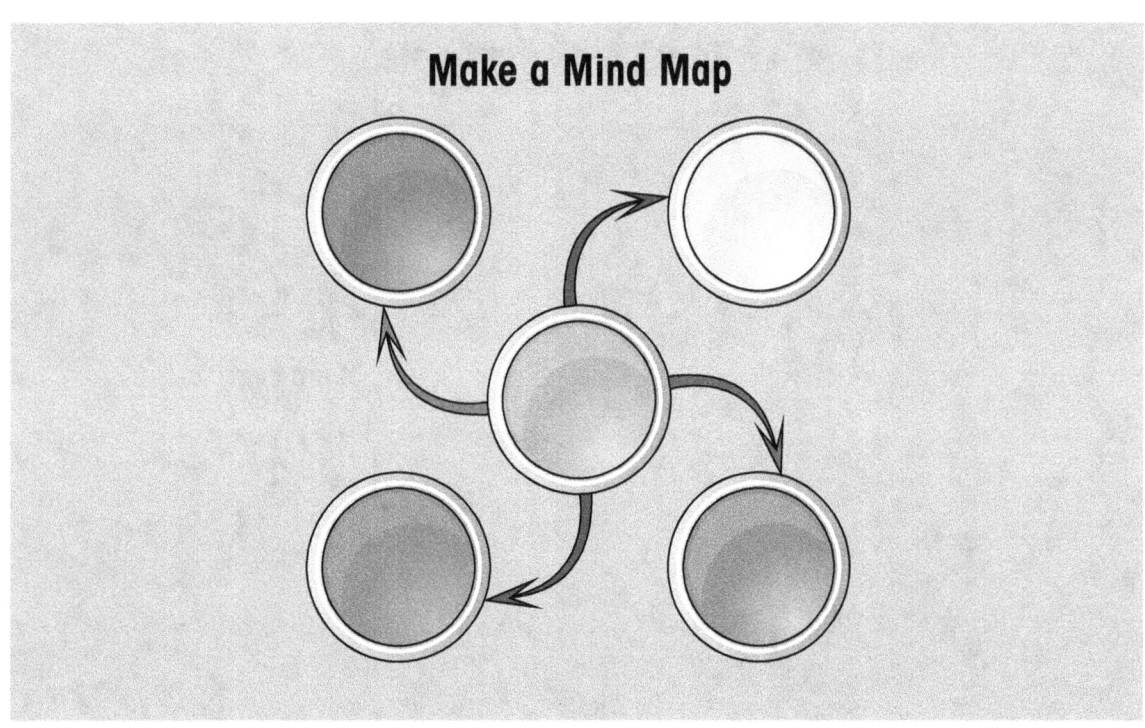

Revision Cards – Visual

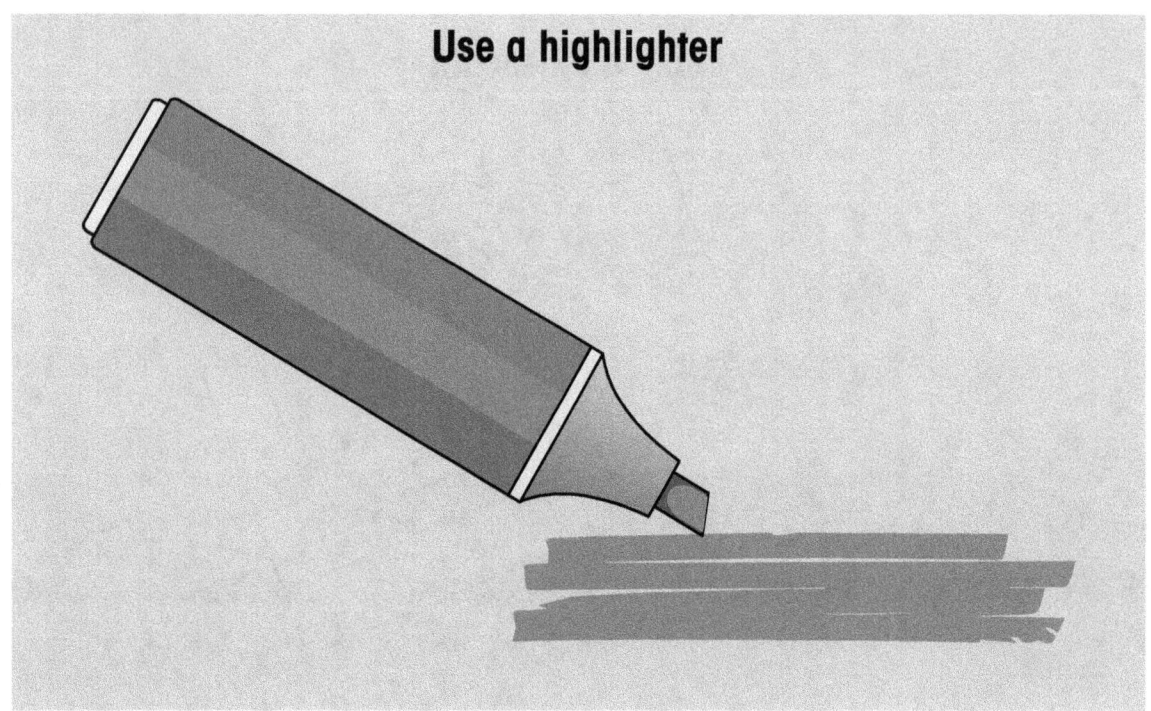

Revision Cards – Visual

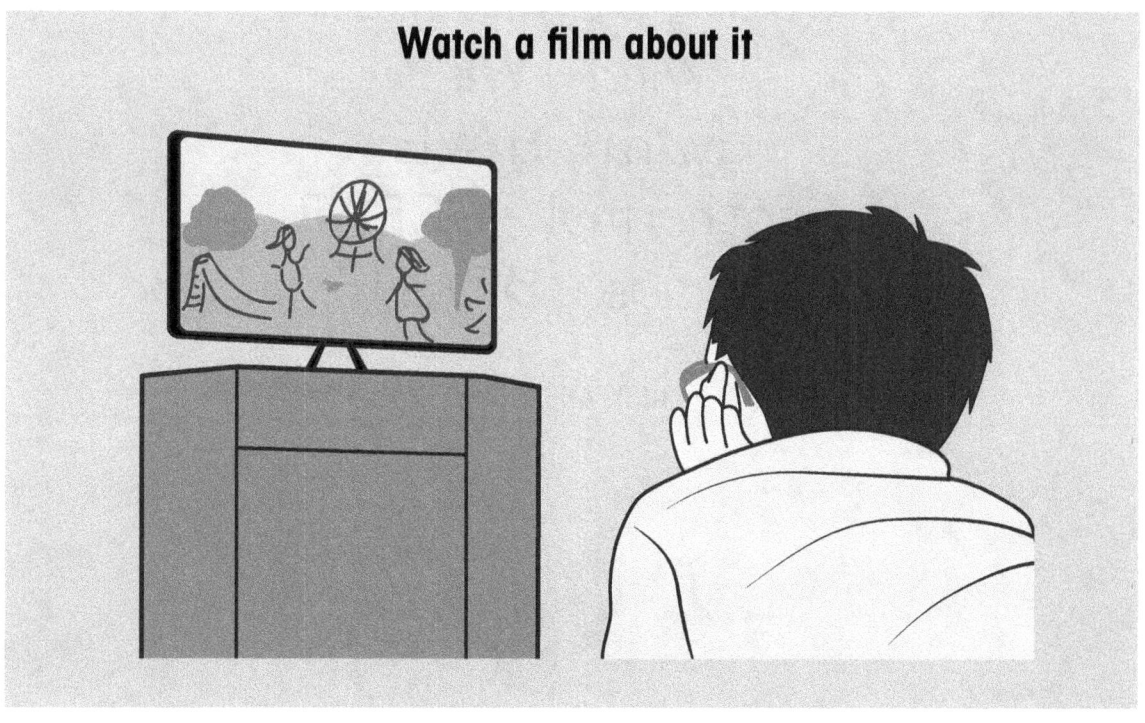

Make a Mnemonic

Here Are Some Popular Mnemonics:

Never **E**at **S**hredded **W**heat
Remembering **North East South West**

Rhythm Helps Your Two Hips Move
Spelling of **Rhythm**

Now let's make our own!

Example: Remember five types of renewable energy:

Solar – **S**OMETIMES
Wind – **W**E
Hydra – **H**AVE
Geothermal – **G**REAT
Biomass – **B**RAINS

Can you think of a better one?

Make a Mnemonic

Auditory (Listening)

Revision Cards – Auditory

(Listening) methods

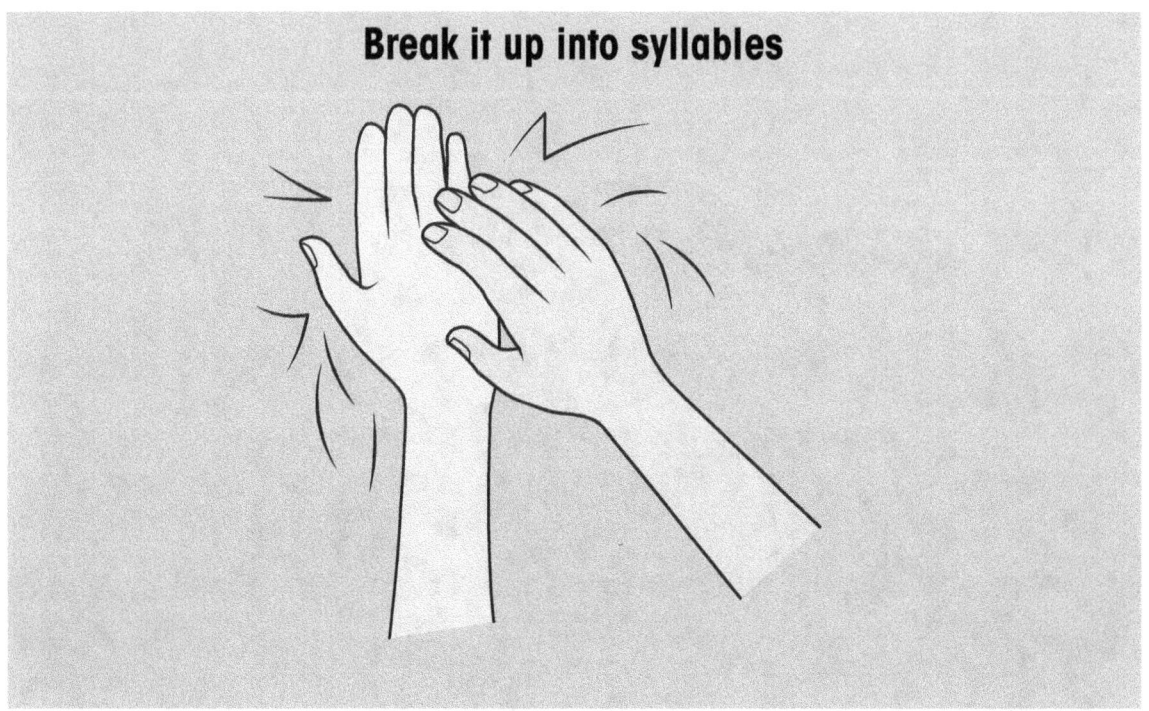
Break it up into syllables

Record it

Revision Cards – Auditory

Revision Cards – Auditory

Make up a sentence with the first letter!

Never Eat Shredded Wheat

For North East South West

Sing it or rap it!

English – Vocabulary 1

Simile	Metaphor	Genre
 As shiny as a star	 He was a giant	

Play	Narrator	Alliteration
		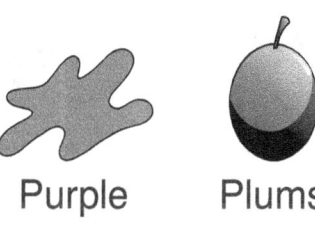 Purple Plums

Rhyme	Personification	Gender
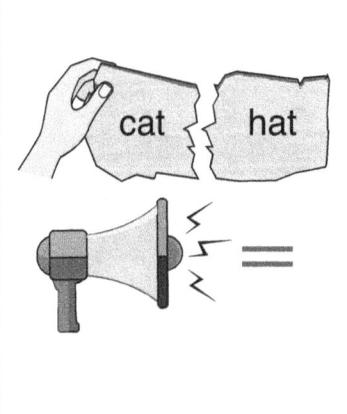	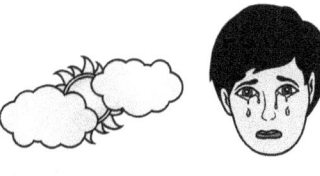 The sky cried	

English – Vocabulary 2

Plot	Biography	Fiction

Mood	Conclusion	Non-Fiction
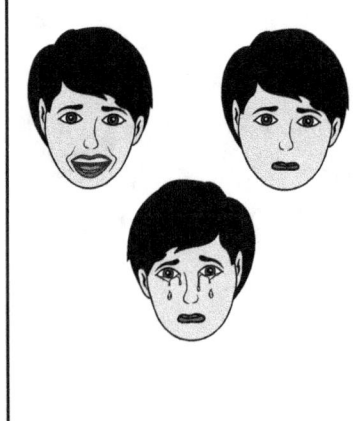		

Fact	Opinion	Autobiography

Maths – Vocabulary 1

Digit	Angle	Horizontal
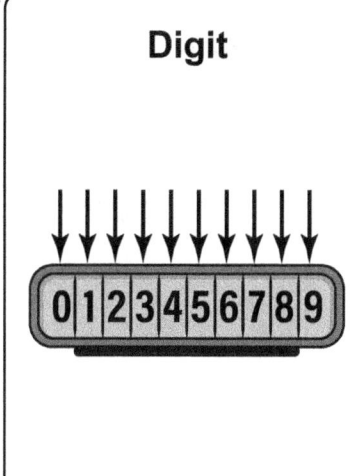	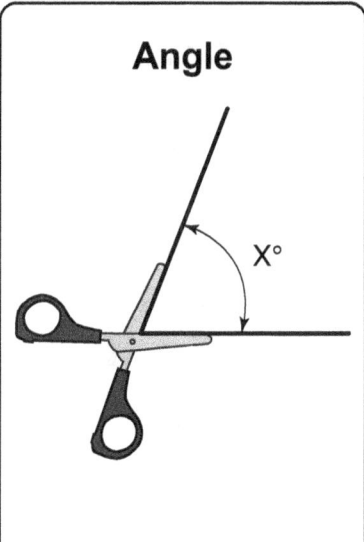	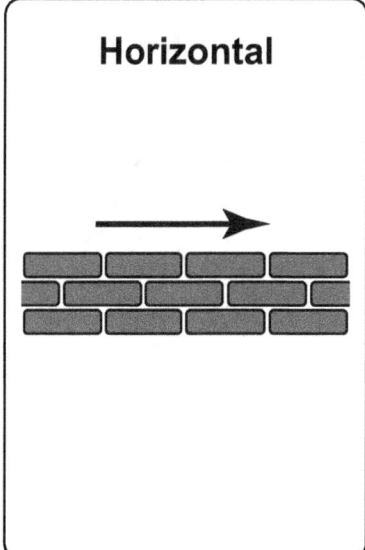

Vertical	Increase	Decrease
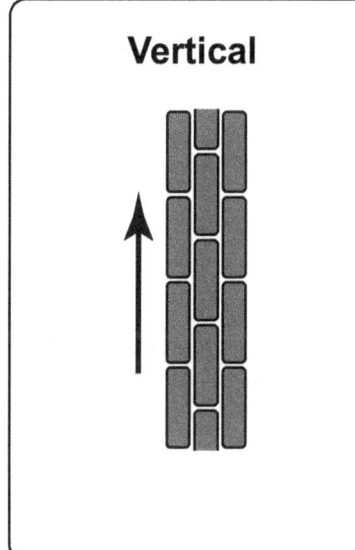	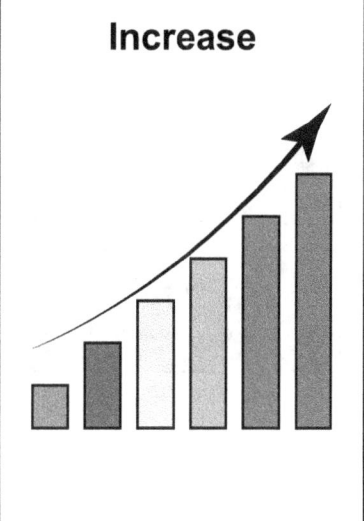	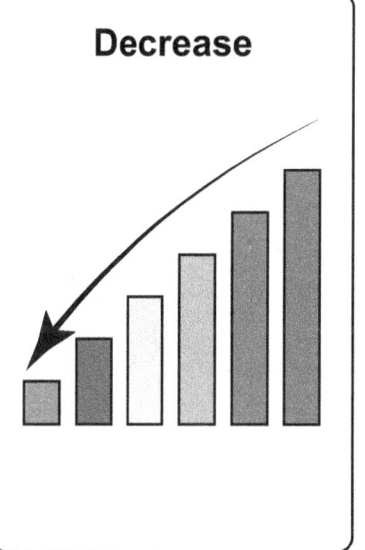

Axis	Parallel	Area
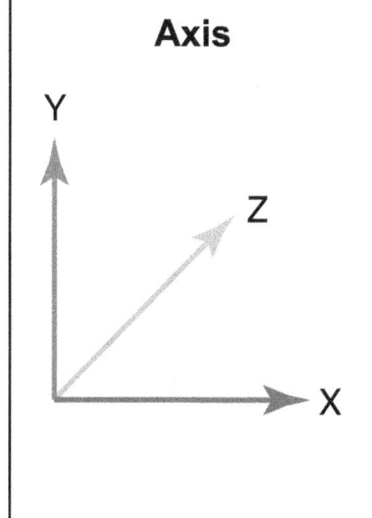	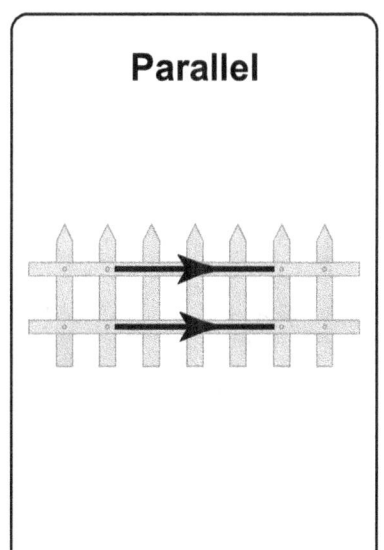	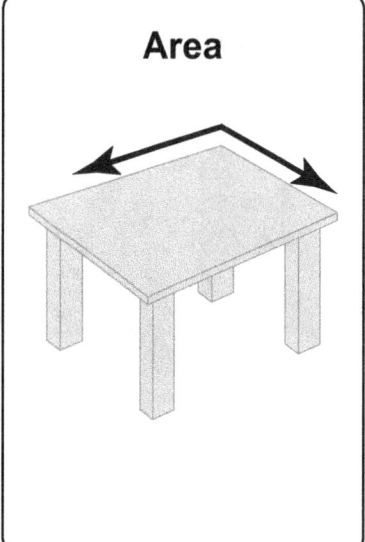

Maths – Vocabulary 2

Circumference	Radius	Diameter
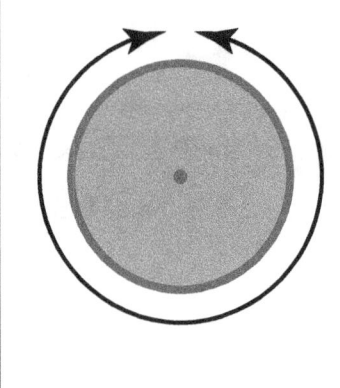	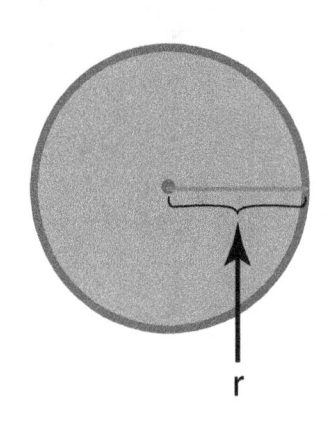	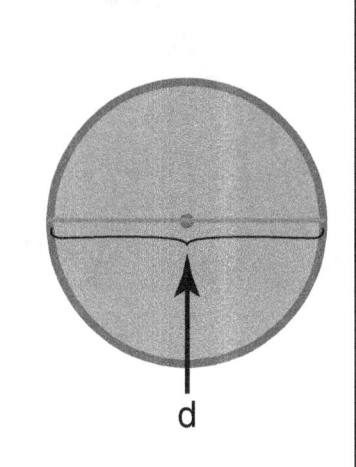

Negative	Formula	Average
	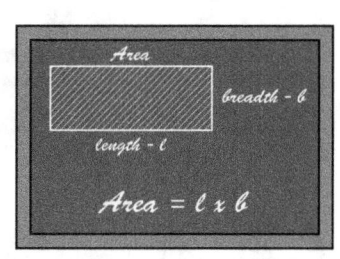	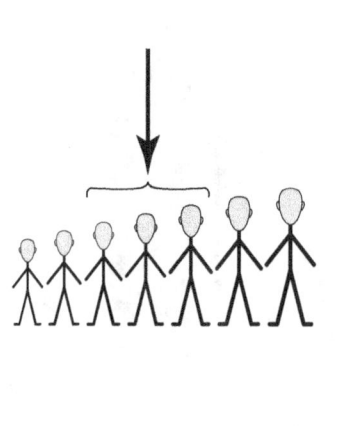

Positive	Equal	Percentage
	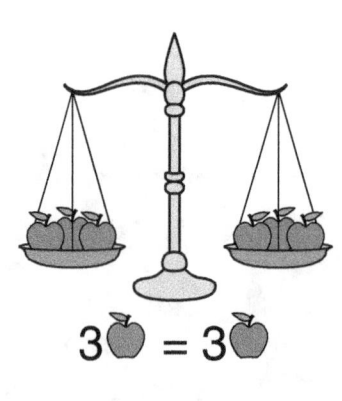	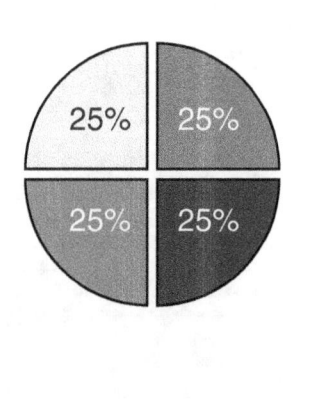

Science – Vocabulary 1

Mammal	Reptile	Amphibian

Respiration	**Circulation**	**Digestion**
	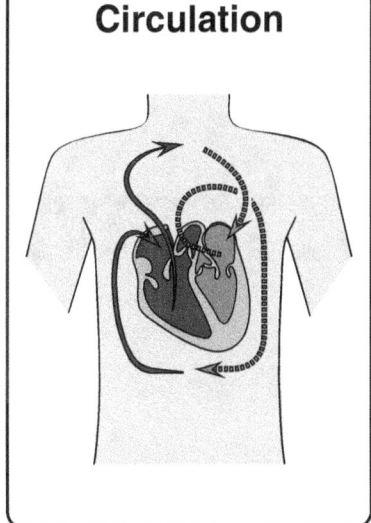	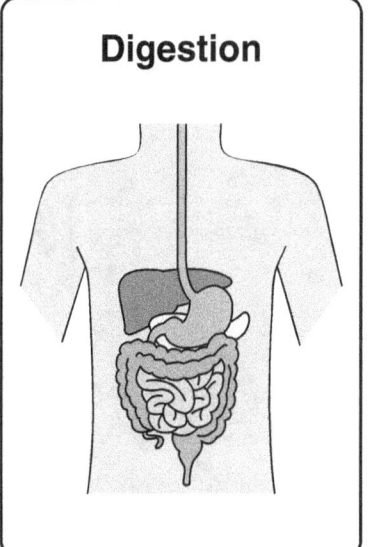
Reproduction	**Gene**	**Nucleus**
	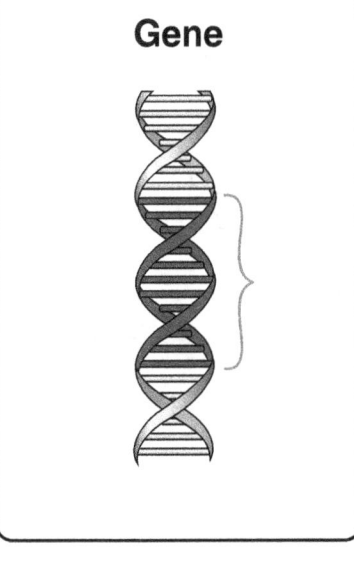	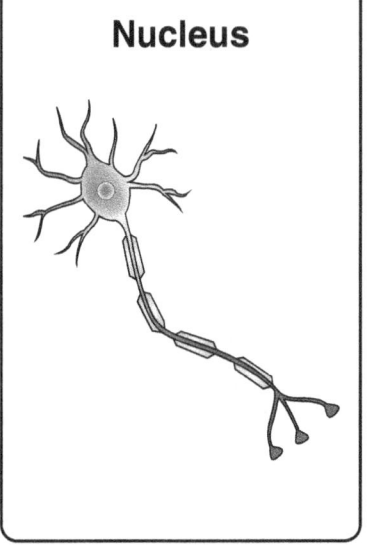

Science – Vocabulary 2

Evaporation	Condensation	Mass
		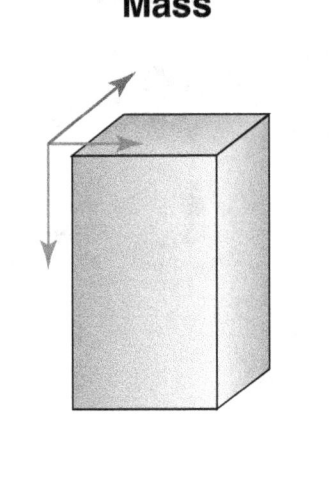

State	Acid	Alkaline
	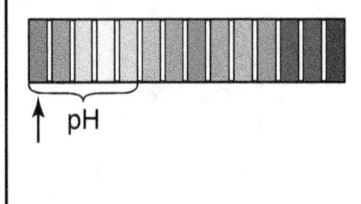	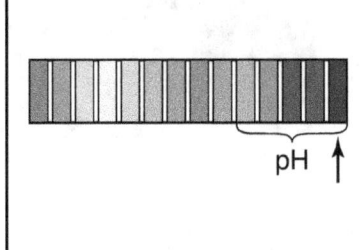

Combustion	Method	Solution
		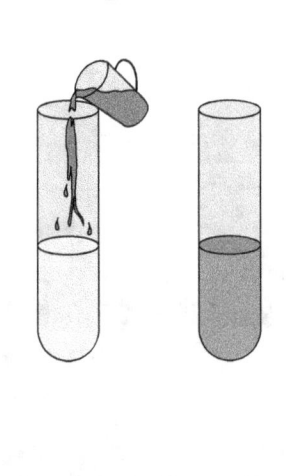

Revision Cards – Kinaesthetic

(Doing) methods

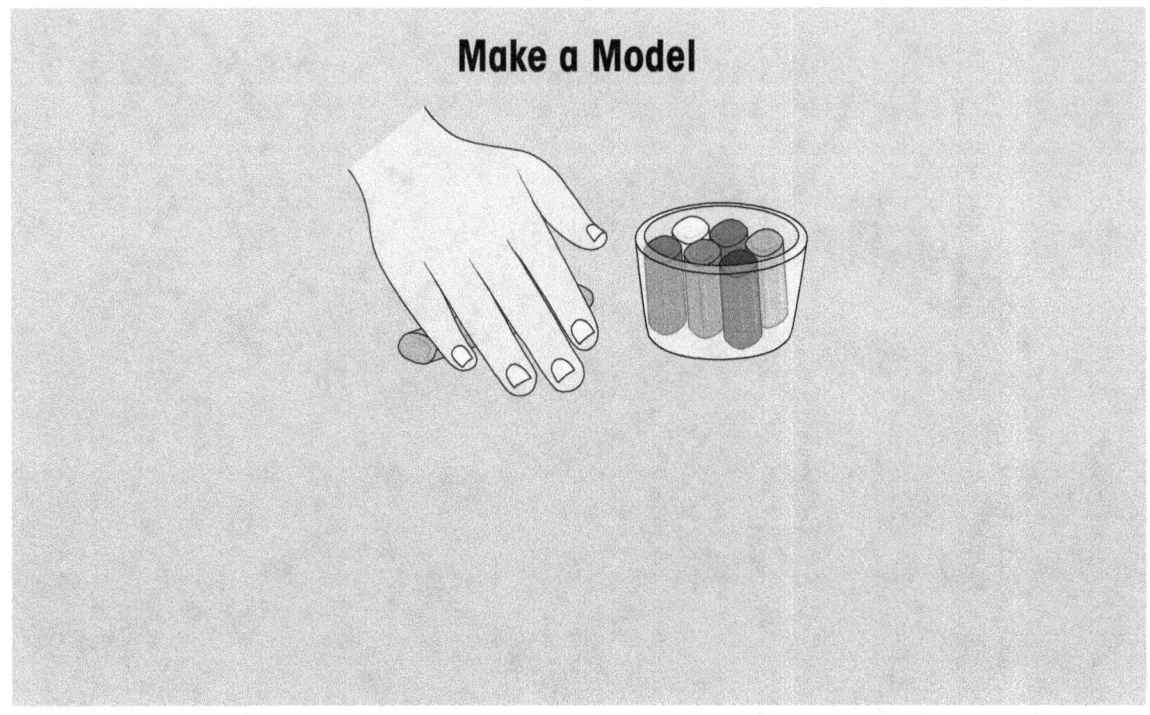

Revision Cards – Kinaesthetic

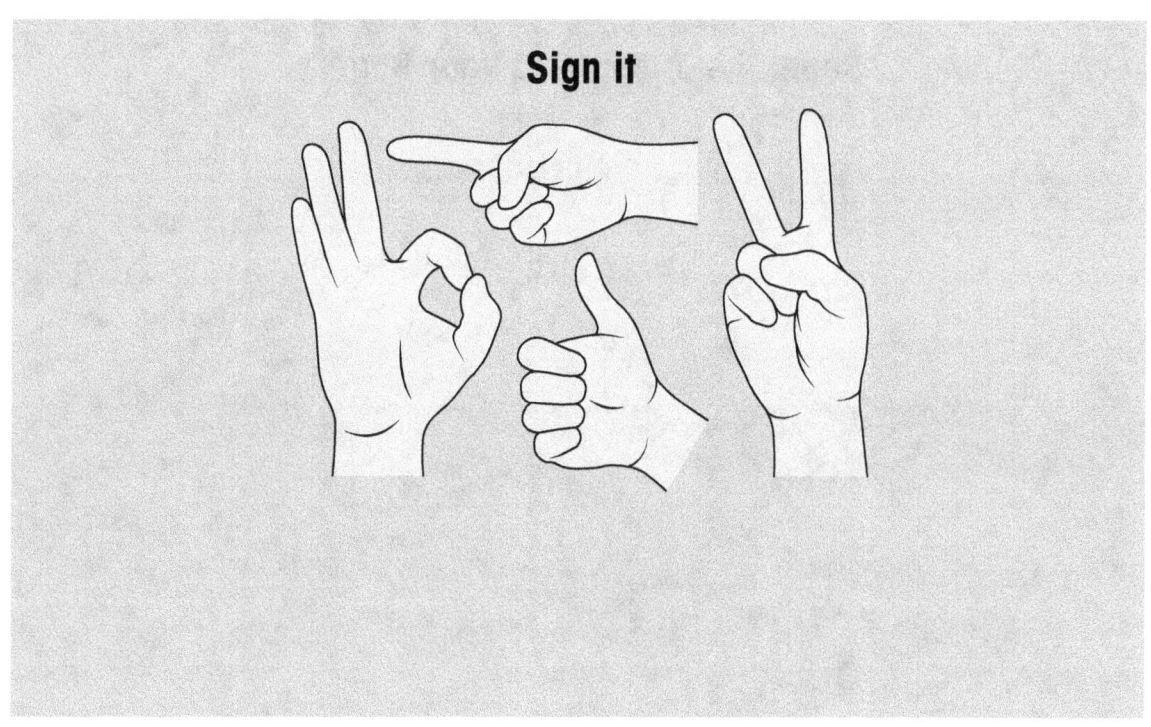

Revision Cards – Kinaesthetic

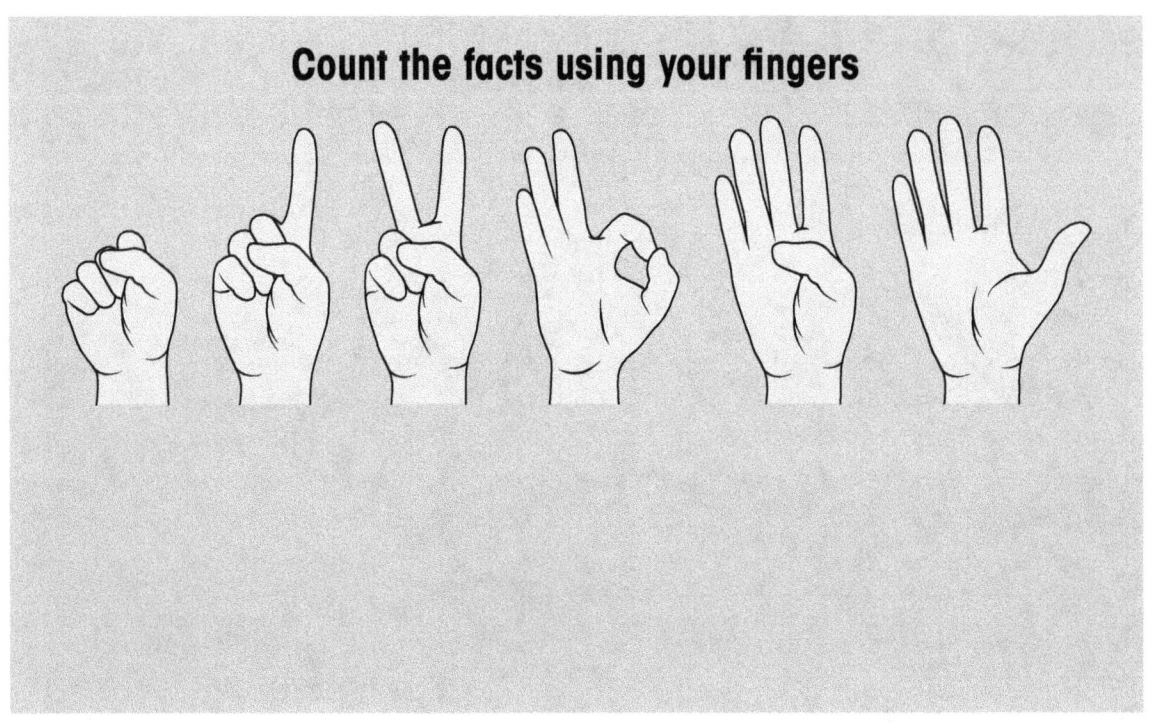

The Time Game

Use examples given or your own:

Making a cup of tea
(5 minutes)

A train from London to Brighton
(58 minutes)

Boil an egg
(6 minutes)

A favourite movie
(The facilitator can choose one that is appropriate to the group,
e.g. Avengers: Endgame (3 hours 2 minutes))

A football match
(90 minutes/1.5 hours)

A song
(The facilitator can choose a familiar song where the time has been noted
and play this in the session)

Revision Timetable

Write in times for revision and study/breaks/relaxation/exercise/rewards or treats
Write in dates/times for exams
Place on fridge/wardrobe at home

	MONDAY	TUESDAY	WEDNESDAY	THURSDAY	FRIDAY	SATURDAY	SUNDAY
MORNING 8.00am to 12.00pm							
AFTERNOON 1.00am to 5.00pm							
EVENING 6.00pm to 10.00pm							

My Timeline

Where are you now? Students mark where they are now on the line.

What happened in the past? Students mark key events in their lives, examples such as when they had their first pet, when they went to primary school, when they met their best friend, when they first travelled on plane.

What are your hopes for the future? Students think of things they may want to do in the future.

Example

Before 0

AGE 10		NOW	AGE 15	AGE 20		AGE 25
Got a pet	Travel the world	Buy a car	Learn a new hobby	Go to college/university	Have a family/children	Get a job

After 25?

Move out · Help the environment

My Timeline: Example

My Timeline

My Timeline

Where are you now?
What happened in the past?
What are your hopes for the future?

Before

0 — AGE 10 — AGE 15 — AGE 20 — AGE 25

After

25?

Exam Words (Command Words)

Cut out the words and definitions:

Students have to match the words according to their meanings

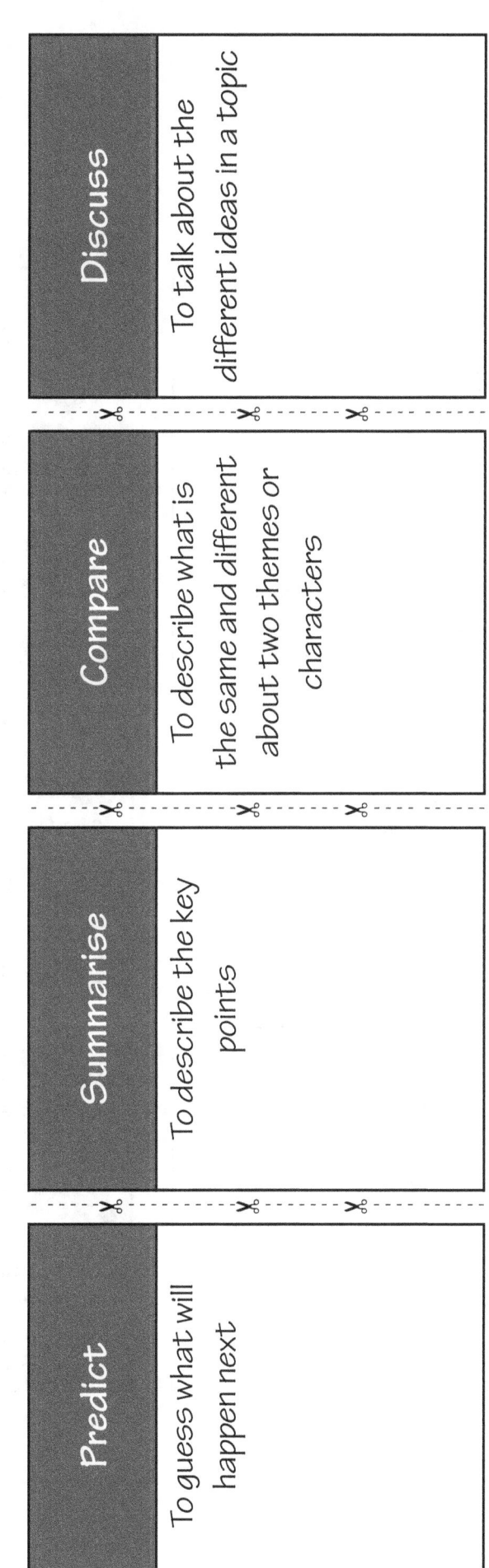

Predict	To guess what will happen next
Summarise	To describe the key points
Compare	To describe what is the same and different about two themes or characters
Discuss	To talk about the different ideas in a topic

Exam Words (Command Words)

Classify — To sort items into different groups

Argue — To say why you believe you are right, giving the other side of the argument too

Analyse — To look at something carefully and look at its detail

Disadvantages — To say why something is bad

Evidence — To give a reason why you think your point is true

Advantages — Say why something is good

Exam Words (Command Words): Word Search

Match the definition next to the word

THEN SEE HOW MANY YOU CAN FIND!!!

Argue
Summarise
Evaluate
Analyse
Justify
Compare
Predict
Estimate

- To say what is the <u>same and different</u> about two things
- To look at the information you have <u>closely</u> and explain everything that might be linked to it
- To explain why something is <u>fair</u> using facts and evidence
- To discuss the <u>value</u> of an idea and all of the different parts of the idea before you reach the conclusion
- To pick out the main bits and write this as <u>summary</u>, e.g. as bullet points
- To give your opinion also thinking about what the opposite opinion is, e.g. in a <u>debate</u>
- To <u>guess</u> what might happen next in an event or story – a word used in English or History lessons
- To <u>guess</u> a number or an amount – a word used in Maths or Science lessons

Exam Words (Command Words): Word Search

C	O	M	P	A	R	E	A	A	B	B	S
V	A	B	C	D	B	S	F	N	O	M	U
J	F	P	E	P	S	T	R	A	T	L	M
U	G	R	P	Q	R	I	S	L	U	K	M
S	H	E	F	G	H	M	H	Y	I	J	A
T	I	D	B	A	A	A	V	S	W	X	R
I	J	I	R	S	W	T	X	E	Y	Z	I
F	K	C	A	C	F	E	G	H	I	J	S
Y	L	T	B	D	E	P	O	N	M	K	E
M	N	O	R	A	R	G	U	E	L	M	P
Q	S	R	T	U	F	G	Y	O	U	W	A
M	E	V	A	L	U	A	T	E	Y	W	O

Argue
Summarise
Evaluate
Analyse
Justify
Compare
Predict
Estimate

# Multiple Meanings

Some words have double meanings!

Can you work out what the double meanings are?

ANGLE	MASS	VOLUME
TABLE	UNIT	CHECK
WAVE	BRACKET	AREA
DIGIT	MEAN	SOLUTION

Multiple Meanings

CAPITAL	DESERT	PRESENT
ROW	WATCH	YARD
SPIRIT	FOOT	FINE
TABLET	STATE	BLOCK
SOURCE	TEXT	DRAW

Being Positive

The facilitator cuts out or verbally shares the statements that are negative with the group. The students change the statements to make them positive. Examples of the positive statements are also given.

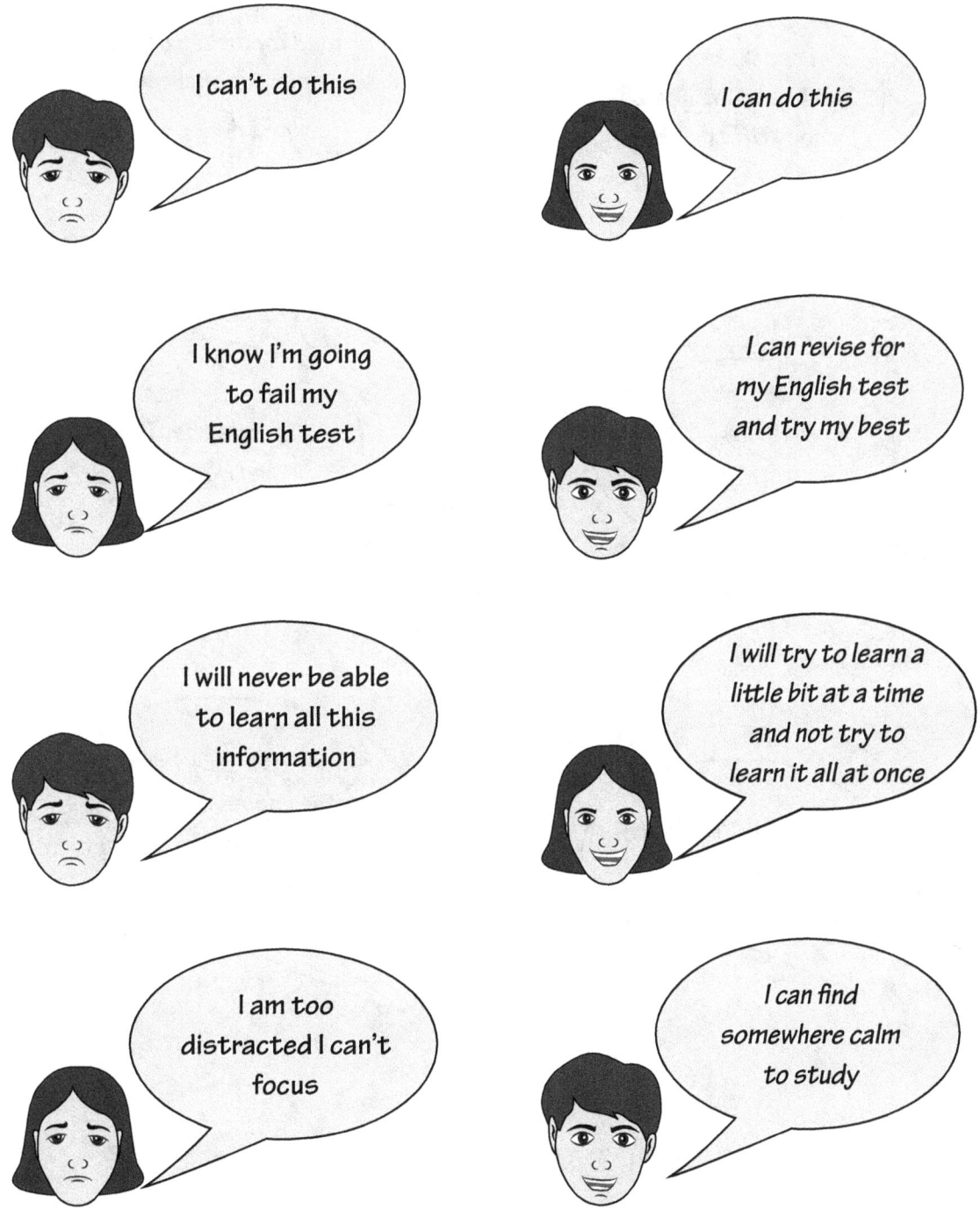

Being Positive

#
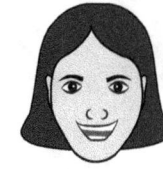

Mindfulness

Hold the orange in your hand and look at it.

Look at it closely!

Look at the colour of the orange, feel the skin of the orange. What does it look like?
It has lots of tiny "pinpricks"; how does the orange skin feel on your fingers?

Put the orange up to your nose and smell it.
Put the orange up to your
ear and shake it; does it make a sound? Keeping the orange to your ear, gently squeeze
the orange with your hand and see if you hear any sound from the inside of the orange.

Now peel the orange and, listen to the sound this makes.
Can you smell it even more?
Is the orange smell getting stronger? If the juice of the orange drips, feel it with your
fingertips – does if feel warm or cold, is the texture sticky or watery?

When it is peeled, look closely at the orange.
Look at the colour
of the inside of the orange;
is it different from the outside?

Mindfulness

As you break open the orange notice the sound it makes as you break it apart into sections.

Take one section of the orange and look at it closely. What can you see? What are the white bits? Are they rough or smooth like the inside? What shape is it now? What do we call this shape? Break one segment open and look at the juice.

Slowly bring the orange to your mouth; is your mouth watering? Watch how your arm moves towards your mouth.

Gently place the orange in your mouth, letting it lie on your tongue first without taking a bite, exploring the feel of the orange in your mouth.

Now bite down on the orange and notice the taste of the orange. Slowly begin to chew the orange and notice which side of the mouth it goes to while you chew.

Feel how it tastes and slowly disappears in your mouth.

Healthy Habits

and foods that help you with your memory!

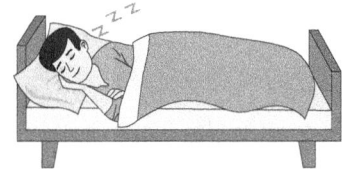

Drink lots of water

Exercise

Sleep at least 8–10 hours per night

Stick to your revision timetable

Make your study space clean, calm and comfortable

Find a quiet space

Use your Study Skills Folder

Omega 3 is good! Eat oily fish/nuts and soybeans

Vitamin E is good! Eat brown rice, oats and sunflower seeds

Berries are good! Put strawberries, blueberries and blackcurrants into milkshakes

Relax and give yourself rewards

Green things are good! Put avocado, kale and broccoli into smoothies

Meditate

Listen to music

Turn off screens

Feed Your Brain

BRAIN-BOOSTING SMOOTHIE

Use this recipe or create your own!

Ingredients

1 banana
½ a cup of fresh or frozen blueberries
½ a cup of fresh or frozen raspberries
½ a cup of walnuts
Fresh apple juice

Equipment Needed

A chopping board
A knife
A blender
A tall glass

1. Peel and chop the banana.
2. Add this to the blueberries, raspberries and walnuts.
3. Put all of the ingredients into a blender.
4. Pour in the apple juice.
5. Blend all the ingredients until they are smooth.

Pour into a glass and drink!

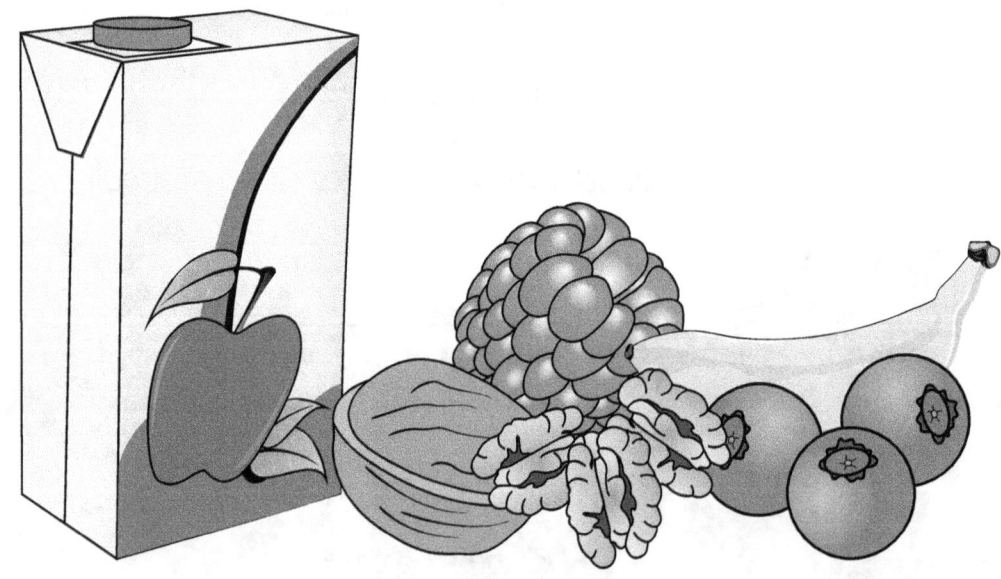

Feed Your Brain

BRAIN-BOOSTING SALAD

Use this recipe or create your own!

Ingredients

1 avocado
4 cups of baby spinach
1 fresh salad tomato
A handful of sunflower seeds or pumpkin seeds
One of these: an oily fish such as salmon or tuna/slice of tofu/cheese (feta or halloumi)/roast chicken/ham slices/boiled egg

Equipment Needed

A salad bowl
A chopping board
A knife

1. Cut the avocado into half, take out the pip and scoop out the middle. Throw the skin and the pip away.
2. Place the soft avocado on a chopping board and cut this into cubes or slices.
3. Add the avocado to the bowl then add the spinach.
4. Slice the tomatoes and then add them to the bowl.
5. Add the protein you have chosen: oily fish (salmon or tuna)/slice of tofu/cheese (feta or halloumi)/roast chicken/ham slices/boiled egg.

Sprinkle the top with sunflower seeds and serve with your favourite dressing!

My Personal Plan

I know how to revise and study for exams.

1--10
😟   🙂

I have learnt two methods that will help me to revise:

1.

2.

If I am stuck I can ask

1_____ for help at school

2_____ for help at home

_____

I have a study skills folder I can save my revision in ☐

I have a revision timetable ☐

When I am stressed I can _____ to help me relax

To be healthy I will _____

I will always try my best! 😎

My Label and Me
Advice sheets for some of the most common SLCN profiles seen in mainstream schools

Autism (ASD)

Can be known as Autistic Spectrum Disorder (ASD) or Autistic Spectrum Condition (ASC). A lifelong condition that affects how a person communicates with and relates to other people, and how they experience the world around them.

Students with autism (ASD) can struggle with:
- Auditory processing and listening skills
- Understanding abstract words and idioms e.g. *'he went through the roof!'* means *'he was angry'*
- Switching topics in conversation
- Meeting new people and changes to routine
- Loud noises, busy environments

However, they are:
- Good at remembering facts, figures and numbers
- Good at focusing on one area, with an excellent eye for detail
- Highly original and inventive thinkers
- Good at working alone
- Perfectionists

Do you understand the words people use to describe this condition?
Do you agree? Disagree?
What else do you know?

Revision and Study Tips

- I can choose Visual (Looking) and Kinaesthetic (Doing) over Auditory (Listening) revision methods.
- I need to keep my study space clear and organised and think about things that might distract me, as I get distracted easily.
- I could use ear defenders or headphones to block out background noise when I'm studying.
- I need to keep to a routine for revision.
- I need to know when and where my exams are, so I feel prepared. I get stressed about exams and I don't like leaving things to the last minute.
- I might practise meditation and add sensory breaks into my revision timetable because I can get anxious sometimes and need time out to chill!

Developmental Language Disorder (DLD)

A lifelong condition that affects language understanding and expression. It is persistent and not linked to another obvious cause.

Students with DLD might struggle with:
- Auditory and short-term memory skills, and remembering words when talking
- Understanding and expressing vocabulary, concepts and grammar correctly
- Understanding and using language appropriately in different social situations
- Using speech sounds

However, they can be:
- Highly sociable, and motivated by rewards
- Good at picking up non-verbal cues from the environment
- Good at maths, art or PE, preferring this over language-based subjects
- Age-appropriate in some areas of language

Do you understand the words people use to describe this condition?
Do you agree? Disagree?
What else do you know?

Revision and Study Tips

- I could choose from lots of revision methods, which include Visual (Looking) Auditory (Listening) and Kinaesthetic (Doing) revision methods.
- I might revise better with someone else and might be better revising with a small group of friends.
- I can try making flashcards and mind maps to help me remember key words. I could use prompts like *Is it a long or short word? How many syllables does it have? Is there a word that rhymes? What does it look like? What is it used for? Where would I find it?* This will help me store the word in my head so I can remember it when I talk and in exams. I am also better at learning when things are visual for me.
- I might give myself a treat when I have done some revision, this will help me work harder.
- I will have to keep going back over my revision as I might forget things quickly. I need to make sure I refer to my Study Skills Folder regularly. I also need extra time to think.

Dyslexia

Dyslexia

A condition also known as a specific learning difficulty that affects the skills involved with accurate and fluent word reading and spelling. This is a lifelong condition and seen as a continuum.

Students with dyslexia might struggle with:
- Reading and spelling
- Short-term memory and recalling sequential facts, e.g. telling time, remembering months of the year, seasons and lists in order
- Expression and using sounds in multisyllabic (long) words
- Time-keeping and organisational skills

However, they can be:
- Good at art, including drawing
- Good at building models and 3D design
- Inventive and good at coming up with original ideas

Do you understand the words people use to describe this condition?
Do you agree? Disagree?
What else do you know?

Revision and Study Tips

- I can choose any revision method that doesn't need me to read and spell.
- I can use my revision timetable to help me remember dates and times, and help me remember the days of the week and months of the year.
- I can keep a watch with me to help me remember the time and to make sure I get to exams on time.
- I need to have regular breaks when I am revising because I get tired very quickly. I also need extra time to think.
- I could keep a spelling chart in my Study Skills Folder to help me with some tricky spellings if I need to write something.
- I could use a Smartpen to help me read some words that are hard, or ask students or adults to help me with my reading.

Dyspraxia (DCD)

Can be known as Developmental Coordination Disorder (DCD). It is a condition that affects fine and gross motor co-ordination. It can also affect expressive language and speech.

A student with dyspraxia struggles with:
- Using the right sounds, words and sentences clearly when talking
- Handwriting and drawing diagrams
- Coordinating physical movements, e.g. dressing, riding a bike
- Time-keeping and organisational skills, having the right equipment

However, they can be:
- Good at understanding verbal language and following non-verbal cues
- Good visually and can notice details others might miss
- Good at empathy and being sociable

Do you understand the words people use to describe this condition?
Do you agree? Disagree?
What else do you know?

Revision and Study Tips

- I could try Visual (Looking) and Auditory (Listening) over Kinaesthetic (Doing) revision methods.
- I need to keep my Study Skills Folder in a safe place and make sure I have all the equipment I need to complete revision at home and at school. I can lose things easily so it might help me to have extra pens and cards in there.
- I need to make sure my revision plan has lots of rest breaks as I can get overtired and anxious. Meditation activities might help me focus better.
- I am not very good at drawing and can find it hard sometimes to make things but I am very visual and I can find pictures and films on the internet to help me with revision.
- I could take photos of objects/lessons of things I need to learn and keep these in my Study Skills Folder for when I need to revise.
- I can be disorganised so having a routine I can stick to throughout the day will help me.

Attention Deficit Hyperactivity Disorder (ADHD)

Attention Deficit Hyperactivity Disorder (ADHD)

A condition where a student has difficulties with attention, hyperactivity and impulsiveness. A subtype of ADHD might also be inattentive (so without hyperactivity) or be a combination of both.

A student with ADHD can struggle with:
- Focusing attention, and concentrating for long periods of time
- Emotional and sensory regulation, e.g. leading to extreme feelings of anxiety, excitement or impulsivity or restlessness
- Time-keeping and organisational skills

However, they can be:
- Highly energetic and passionate
- Focused when they are doing an activity they enjoy
- Creative thinkers
- Good at multitasking

Do you understand the words people use to describe this condition?
Do you agree? Disagree?
What else do you know?

Revision and Study Tips

- I could try Kinaesthetic (Doing) revision methods as I have lots of energy and need movement.
- Revision and study times need to be short. I get bored easily.
- I need to make sure I get lots of sleep and think about my diet. Fizzy drinks and sugar can be bad for me as they make it harder for me to concentrate.
- I need to make sure my study environment is quiet and not distracting.
- I might add a fidget toy in my Study Skills Folder. I might also put some headphones in there so that I can block out noise when I'm revising.
- I might take a stopwatch or timer into exams with me where the passing of time is visible, so that I don't get anxious about having too much or too little time left in the exam.

Appendices

Parent Letter Template 106

Warm-up Games 107

Session Plan: Study Skills Group 111

Revision and Study Skills 112

Parent Letter Template

Dear Parents

This is a letter to inform you that _____ will be accessing a revision and study skills group at _____. The aim of the group is to help them to learn revision and study methods that build on their learning strengths so that they feel more confident when approaching homework, revision and exams.

The group is split into 10 key areas which include learning about different revision methods linked to visual, auditory and kinaesthetic ways of learning, making a revision timetable, understanding time, following complex words and command words in exam questions, and knowing what to expect in exams. The group will also cover aspects such as developing a healthy lifestyle and how to deal with stress, focusing mainly on students being positive about themselves and about them developing confidence.

Furthermore, they will be able to interact and develop their communication skills in a safe learning space with similar students whilst working towards improving their individual studying skills both at home and in school.

Each session has a follow-up activity, so that they are able to generalise some of their skills outside of the group. It is hoped that the follow-up activity can therefore be supported at home to maximise their chances of success.

For more information please contact _____

Thank you for your support

Kind regards

Warm-up Games

Session 1 Spin the Bottle

There are 10 statements to cut out. Spin a bottle or choose a card, the student answers to:

1 What is your favourite pet?
2 Where was your best holiday?
3 What is your favourite food?
4 Who is your best friend?
5 What makes you scared?
6 What do you like to do at the weekend?
7 Do you have any brothers and sisters?
8 What is your worst food?
9 What is your best movie?
10 What is your favourite hobby?

Session 2 Senses Bag – Pass the Object

What are our five senses? Look/Listen/Touch/Taste/Smell

Fill a bag with a range of objects which link to a range of senses, e.g. a stress ball (touch), a flashlight (sight), coffee (smell), a sliced lemon (taste), a bell (sound).

Pass the object and try to encourage the students to think of as many descriptive words as they can to define the touch, sight, smell, taste and sound of the object. Start with a new student and object when the list of words has been exhausted for each new object.

Vocabulary they can use can include soft/hard/gooey/rough/bright/colourful/sparkly/shiny/bitter/strong/sour/sweet/loud/calming/quiet/gentle

Warm-up Games

Session 3 Spot the Difference

This can be done as a paper exercise (taken from an external source, e.g. Internet) or this could be a visual game where the facilitator and student go out of the room, change one aspect of the way they look and the rest of the group must guess what is different!

> Examples of changes might be: The student puts on or takes off a scarf, a hat or a glove or they pull a sock up over the trouser or they put their collars up or down or they wear their hair differently. The rest of the group spot the changes as quickly as they can

Session 4 Syllable Race

The facilitator gives a category, e.g. things that fly.

The student must think of a word that belongs in the category, e.g. "helicopter", "rocket". The syllables for each word given are added and the student with the highest number wins.

> (This could also link in with the current curriculum topic/theme to make the game more relevant or functional, e.g. *Describe the character of Macbeth? Ambitious, Guilty, Powerful*)

Session 5 Find the Shape

A game to reinforce concepts linked to size and shape.

Using modelling clay, the facilitator creates model shapes that are long/short/fat/thin/spiral/flat and places them under a piece of cloth. This could also be adapted to circle/square/triangle/rectangle/oval/cube.

The students must try and name the shape through just touch.

Session 6 Time Game – Categories

Choose a category. Students must think of as many items that belong in that category as possible in 10 seconds. The facilitator will need a stopwatch for this exercise.

> Examples: Famous cartoon characters/Wild animals/Sweet foods/Cheesy foods/Green things/Types of weather/Underwater creatures/Types of transport/Ball games/UK cities, etc.

Warm-up Games

Session 7 Word Definition Game

Before the students come into the room, a keyword is placed on a sticky note attached to the back of their chair. This can be taken from the curriculum vocab list or be linked to something they need to revise.

They must define the word before the session starts.

If they don't know the word, they must think of something they might do to find out! E.g. they could ask someone or use a dictionary or the Internet.

> (The facilitator places dictionaries or has a tablet/PC connected nearby so that they know they can use this to look up their answers.)

Session 8 Music

The facilitator chooses a piece of calming, soothing music which is played as students walk into the room, e.g. classical music.

Notice students' reactions. Allow them to take their seats. Try not to say or do anything for at least 5 minutes after they walk in.

Now give them a piece of paper and ask them to try and draw a picture or verbally describe how that music might have made them feel, or what it makes them think of, e.g. calming, relaxed, made them think of being in a park, on a beach. Prompt for answers. It's ok too if the music did not evoke any emotion or feeling!

The facilitator can then talk about how It's ok that we don't *all* feel the same and that music can affect us in different ways.

Session 9 Paper Plates

An introduction to healthy and non-healthy food. A paper plate is given to each student. The students are asked to draw/colour or paste a picture from a magazine of an item of food that they think is healthy, nutritious and will help feed their brain.

They pair up and describe what is on their plate to a partner who must guess the items on their plate. The student can only answer to yes and no questions, e.g.: Is it green? (yes) Is it sweet (yes) Is it crunchy (yes) Does it grow on trees? (yes)

The student then guesses: Is it an apple?

Warm-up Games

Session 10 — Compliments Game

The students must share one compliment with the facilitator about each member of the group who writes this down. The individual student is then allowed to hear the individual comments that have been written about him or her and say WHO in the group might have said this comment about them.

Session 10 — Compliments Game

Session Plan: Study Skills Group

Date:

Name	Activity	Comment

Revision and Study Skills

Definition of Terms

Revision

These are the strategies that allow the student to engage with what they learn so that they can recall it and use it later either in coursework or an exam.

Here they are going over information to understand it, making links to other learning they have done already.

The strategies students choose to revise could be Visual, Auditory or Kinaesthetic, or could incorporate more than one modality and not necessarily be all three.

Study Skills

These are the skills that students can develop over time so they get the maximum benefit from revision and learning; e.g. **Make a Flashcard** is an effective visual method of learning new information but the student will struggle to use this if:

a) They are tired, anxious, feeling restless or feeling low
b) They do not have anywhere to study, or the study area is too dark, noisy, hot or cluttered
c) They do not have the correct materials to hand to enable them to make a flashcard

Study skills are therefore how we manage this.

Evidence shows that for revision and study skills to be effective all areas need to be considered: the student, their methods, their studying environments, their health, their mental wellbeing and the support they have around them.

Advice for Educators when supporting Students with the Revision and Study Skills Programme

- Always make sure the student has a key person they can go to for help when studying. They should be able to identify a key person at home or at a school who they feel comfortable with, e.g. a parent or a tutor.
- Make sure there is plenty of time to revise and study before upcoming exams, so that the student is well prepared.
- Do not "force" revision and study time. Be gentle and accepting that the student may not be in the right state of mind due to feeling tired, distracted or overwhelmed.
- Negotiate with the student and let them give you an alternative time where they might feel more able to focus and work in their learning environment.
- Try to encourage students to make a revision plan with clear breaks for rewarding activities, rest and exercise built in.
- Encourage students to keep revision times short, e.g. 20–30 minutes. 30 minutes is enough time to start a simple mind map. You can always go back to the map after a break and add more!
- Encourage students to be creative and inventive with their learning.
- Let students present their information in a variety of ways and showcase pieces they have done, e.g. taking photos of mind maps, placing some Revision Cards on a dedicated wall in an area where they and others can see what they have done.
- Recognise and reinforce effort and success by "process" praise (praise for efforts) and not based on how good/bad an outcome is.

    E.g. saying, *"You wrote the word JUSTIFY in BIG letters using BRIGHT colours This will help you remember that word! Well done"* rather than saying, *"That's a great flashcard!"*

- Check the student's attention and focus before you start any revision sessions. Use a game or activity that lets you gain their auditory attention first. This could be as simple as choosing a word they need to learn and cutting out the letters, so they rebuild the word from the letters they are given. Your sessions with that student are much more likely to be successful if you have got their attention right at the start.
- Ensure that the student makes good use of their Study Skills Folders. Let them personalise these and add additional things that they know help them to learn, e.g. a spelling chart, fidget toy, magnets, headphones and anything else that might support their learning.
- Refer back to their Personal Plans regularly and check the revision methods they are using, breaking this down if needed into **Visual, Auditory and Kinaesthetic** methods to give the pupil the maximum opportunity to learn new vocabulary, concepts, ideas and information.

Revision and Study Skills

- Ensure that there are regular opportunities to reuse/recap key vocabulary they need to learn across the day and in different subjects to help them learn new words and complex words.
- Remember many curriculum words will have double meanings so always ensure that this is made as explicit as possible when teaching or supporting students with vocabulary.
- Provide pictures the students can cut out if they are unable to draw themselves. Support all written words with visual information where possible to reinforce any learning.
- Always reinforce that there is no such thing as "perfect" but it is about "trying one's best".
- Give the student choices on what to revise, where to revise, who to revise with and how long to revise.
- The student should feel in control of their learning, even if this is not something that you do all the time. Empower the student by letting them make some of their own decisions.
- Try to involve the parents and caregivers by ensuring that they know the procedures for exams and what the student is required to learn. Parents' and caregivers' involvement will enable the student to feel supported and will allow parents to feel involved in their child's learning.
- Talk about how good it feels to be UNIQUE and DIFFERENT and talk about those icons in history who have managed to overcome personal challenges and become successful.
- Having a wall with positive role models in history or the media that is visible is also a way to support students with developing their own identities and self-esteem.
- Use the My Label and Me advice sheets as ways to support young students who have a diagnosis with understanding their diagnosis better. Talk about the strengths that are inherent in their differences and in the way they might learn compared to other students.

Bibliography

AFASIC (2009) "Unlocking Speech and Language Including Young People with Speech, Language and Communication Difficulties in Secondary School". AFASIC Publications. London.

Beard, Jenni (2007) *Speedy Study Skills – Learn the Skills with the Minimum of Reading: A Quick Multisensory Guide for Students.* Crossbow Education. Stafford UK.

Denworth, Lydia (2019) "Debate Arises over Teaching Growth Mindsets to Motivate Students. Research Shows the Conflicting Data on the Impact of the Intervention, but a Major New Study Confirms It Can Work", *Scientific American.* https://www.scientificamerican.com/article/debate-arises-over-teaching-growth-mindsets-to-motivate-students.

Dockerill, Julie, Peter Howell, Diane Leung & Andrew J. B. Fugard (2017) "Children with Speech, Language and Communication Needs in England: Challenges for Practice", *Frontiers in Education,* Vol. 2, No. 35. pp. 1–14.

Doidge, Norman (2008) *The Brain that Changes Itself – Stories of Personal Triumph from the Frontiers of Science.* London: Penguin.

Garcier, Susan (2018) *Mindful Kids: the Complete Guide to Help Your Child Focus and Succeed in Life.* Independently published.

Gettinger, M (2002) "Contributions of Study Skills to Academic Competence", *Seibert School Psychology Review,* Vol. 31, No. 3, pp. 350–365.

Gross, J. (2017) *Time to Talk – Implementing Outstanding Practice in SLT.* 2nd edn. Abingdon: Routledge.

Hoover, J. J. (1989) "Study Skills and the Education of Students with Learning Disabilities", *Journal of Learning Disabilities,* Vol. 22, No. 7, pp. 452–5, 461.

Ripley, Kate & Jenny Barrett (2008) *Supporting Speech and Language Needs.* London: Sage.

Snowling, Margaret, Hannah Nash & Lisa Henderson (2008) "The Development of Literacy Skills in Children with Down Syndrome: Implications for Intervention", *Down Syndrome Research and Practice,* No. 12. Down Syndrome Research and Practice Advance Online Publication: www.down-syndrome.org/research.

Woliver, Jessica (2009) *Alphabet Kids from ADD to Zellweger Syndrome.* London: Jessica Kingsley.

Websites

www.afasic.org.uk
www.dldandme.org
www.thecommunicationtrust.org.uk
www.talkingpoint.org
www.ican.org.uk
www.naplic.org.uk
www.nasen.org.uk
www.radld.org
www.youngminds.org.uk
www.dyspraxiafoundation.org.uk
www.autism.org.uk
www.dyslexiafoundation.org.uk
www.themindfulnessinitiative.org
www.bercow10yearson.com
www.bebrainfit.com

Revision websites/Apps

www.khanacademy.org
www.quizlet.com
www.gojimo.com
www.getrevising.co.uk
www.bbc.co.uk/bitesize

For Product Safety Concerns and Information please contact our EU
representative GPSR@taylorandfrancis.com
Taylor & Francis Verlag GmbH, Kaufingerstraße 24, 80331 München, Germany

www.ingramcontent.com/pod-product-compliance
Lightning Source LLC
Chambersburg PA
CBHW080833010526
44112CB00015B/2501